D1328767

Nathan the Wise

by Gotthold Ephraim Lessing
Translated from the German
Nathan der Weise

by Stephanie Clennell and Robert Philip

First published in 1992 by

The Open University
Walton Hall
Milton Keynes
United Kingdom
MK7 6AA

ISBN 0 7492 1112 1

Acknowledgements

Frontispiece Gotthold Ephraim Lessing. (Mansell Collection)

Edited, designed and typeset by The Open University.

This book forms part of an Open University course A206 *The Enlightenment.*

Printed and bound in Great Britain by Bell and Bain Ltd, Glasgow
1.2

4563C/a206nti1.1

Contents

G. E. Lessing.

Introduction
Gotthold Ephraim Lessing, 1729–81

The young scholar

Lessing was born in 1729 in the small town of Kamenz in the Protestant state of Saxony. His family background was Lutheran and academic. His father, Johann Gottfried Lessing, was chief pastor of the main church in Kamenz. Johann Lessing had studied at the University of Wittenberg and kept up his academic interest by writing and translating theological works, but he had a large family and was very poor. He applied successfully to the Elector of Saxony for a scholarship for his eldest son, Gotthold Ephraim, to attend the prestigious electoral school (Fürstenschule) of St Afra in Meissen.

St Afra had high academic standards. Life there was austere, with an emphasis on religious observance. The young Lessing thrived on the rigorous classical training, and impressed his teachers with his intellect and independence of mind.

When Lessing left the school in 1746 he became a student of Protestant theology at the University of Leipzig, as his parents wished. At first he devoted himself to study, as he had done at school, but then in Leipzig 'a place where one can see the whole world in miniature' he began to realize that he needed to educate himself for living in society. He wrote in a long letter to his mother: 'I learned what a difference there was between me and other people. A timid country lad, a clumsy, graceless body, complete ignorance of manners ... I felt a sort of shame that I had never felt before.'[1]

He learned to dance, fence and ride; and he discovered the theatre. At that time a theatre company run by the formidable Karoline Neuber[2] was presenting plays in Leipzig, including translations of classical French plays. Lessing became passionately interested in the theatre. He wrote a play *The Young Scholar* ('Der junge Gelehrte') which was successfully performed by the Neuber company in 1748. His lifelong active interest in the theatre had begun, and at the same time led to the first

---

[1] 20 January 1749. Vol XVII no.6 in Lachmann-Muncker edn. of Lessing's *Sämtliche Schriften* (complete writings), 3rd edn. Berlin, Stuttgart and Leipzig, 1886–1924. Letters: vols XVII–XXI.

[2] Karoline Neuber (1697–1760) was well educated and of good family. She escaped from a cruel and tyrannical father by eloping with a young student, whom she married in 1718. Their only recourse was to join a theatrical troupe and some years later Karoline was managing her own company.

disputes with his parents. They were worried, horrified even, by this worldly interest. Indeed to strict Lutherans the theatre was anathema (a point briefly referred to in *Nathan the Wise*). Lessing respected his parents' views, and he remained, in his way, a dutiful son. He did not see his developing independence of thought as a revolt against them, but rather wanted to make them understand his own changing outlook, including his wish to give up the study of theology. This need to come to terms with his own and other people's views on religion lasted all his life, as you will find when you read *Nathan the Wise*.

With his father's reluctant approval Lessing changed to the study of medicine and philology. He did not complete his studies in Leipzig, because he had to make a quick escape. The Neuber theatre company was in debt and disbanded. Lessing had imprudently acted as surety for some of the actors; he was in no position to provide any money, and went secretly to the University of Wittenberg. 'For the first and only time in his life he was guilty of a dishonourable action' said H.B. Garland (1962, p.9).

Lessing enrolled as a medical student in Wittenberg, but fell ill, and gave up his studies after a few months and went to Berlin. He had decided that he would try to live as a writer in Berlin. There would be for him no respectable career as a pastor or university teacher, as his parents had hoped; instead he would face hardship, insecurity and poverty. But he would be independent.

The spread of Enlightenment

In 1748 it was just possible to make a living by writing. Johnson in England, and Diderot in France, are notable examples of this. There was a growing demand for literary works to which publishers responded. In the German states, periodicals, the so-called 'moral weeklies', began to appear in the 1720s, following the example of the English *Tatler*, *Spectator*, and *Guardian*. There were hundreds of these periodicals by the 1760s, although the life-span of each was short (about three years). More specialized periodicals also appeared, such as learned journals (which had appeared in Latin in the seventeenth century) and literary and political periodicals. It was through these that 'the process of the enlightenment as an overall movement began', according to Aner (1929, p.30).

Lessing was well equipped to take part in this movement. He had had a sound academic training and people like him could earn a little money by writing, editorial work, private teaching or translation. Lessing widened his own knowledge of works, especially contemporary ones, in English, French and Spanish, as well as German. He had a talent for publicity. He made the most of speedy and frequent publication, so that his writings and his ideas spread quickly among the enlightened élites in the various German states. From 1751 he was an editor of the Berlin Gazette (the *Berliner priviligierte Zeitung*) and its monthly supplements, and was cited as an important critic.[3] With like-minded friends in Berlin he was able to carry on a campaign for enlightened ideas. As this stage this meant questioning, analysing and criticizing existing ideas and works. He was relentlessly critical of Professor Johann Christoph Gottsched's[4] attempts to improve German literature, particularly drama, by insisting on close imitation of French classical literature of the seventeenth century. Instead Lessing put forward other models, such as Shakespeare, and introduced new works and ideas to the reading public in Germany. For example, Rousseau's essay the *Discourse on the Arts and Sciences* appeared in 1750, and Lessing reviewed this work (and questioned its assumptions) just a few months later, in April 1751.

Lessing was ready to take risks, stir up trouble, and criticize the eminent. As a critic he was intent on raising standards, as someone who '... does not deny the truth in order to flatter, is convinced that a warning about a bad book is a service which one renders to the public, one which is more worthy of an honest man than a servile facility for bartering praise for praise' (*Letters on modern literature, Briefe die neueste Litteratur betreffend*, 1759).

His attacks were specific and the most eminent contemporaries were not spared. '... and Voltaire's *Zaire?* How inferior it is to the *Moor of Venice* (*Othello*) of which it is a poor copy.'[5] Lessing's contacts with Voltaire (Frederick the Great's guest in Berlin from 1750–53) were mainly unfortunate. He had done some translation for Voltaire, notably of his *History of the Crusades*. A friend, Richier de Louvain, Voltaire's secretary, had lent the proofs of Voltaire's *Age of Louis XIV* (*Siècle de Louis XIV*) to Lessing, who carelessly took them with him when he went to Wittenberg in 1751. Voltaire was outraged, suspected a pirating attempt, and complained to Frederick, who did not forget the incident.

Lessing's reason for returning to Wittenberg was to get his Master's degree. He was successful, and returned to Berlin in 1752 to work again for the *Berliner priviligierte Zeitung.*

Friends and allies

Berlin was now an important centre of serious literary criticism. There was relative freedom of expression (except in writing about politics and

---

[3] 'A new critic has appeared here whose work you will be able to judge from the enclosed review of *The Messiah* (Klopstock's epic poem). He just seems a little young.' J.J. Sulzer to J.J. Bodmer (in R. Daunicht (1971) *Lessing im Gespräch*, München.

[4] Gottsched (1700–66) *Versuch einer Critischen Dichtkunst für die Deutschen* (*Essay on the Art of Poetry for Germans*, 1730).

[5] *Letters on modern literature* No.17, 1759.

the State, as Lessing said in a later acid comment).[6] Lessing had a circle
of friends among writers, booksellers and publishers. In 1754 he met two
men who became his lifelong friends and with whom he worked closely
in Berlin. They were Friedrich Nicolai[7] (1733–1811), a writer and book-
seller, and Moses Mendelssohn[8] (1729–86), whom he first met as a chess-
player. In October 1754 Lessing wrote of Mendelssohn: '[He] is actually
a Jew, aged about 20, who, without any education, has a remarkable
grasp of languages, mathematics, philosophy and poetry. I expect him to
become an honour to his nation, if he is allowed to develop fully, unlike
those of his religion who are always driven by a terrible spirit of per-
secution.'[9]

Moses Mendelssohn was the son of a public scribe in Dessau. He
had been taught by a rabbi, and when the rabbi went to Berlin, Moses, at
the age of 14, followed him there, determined to educate himself and
live as best he could by copying and teaching. As a Jew he had very few
rights even in Frederick the Great's Prussia. Jews still had a separate and
subordinate legal status. Some few had a special status as protected Jews
(*Schutzjuden*). In 1753 Frederick revised the regulations about Jews, but
mainly in order to make use of a small number of wealthy Jews as manu-
facturers and bankers. In 1749 Lessing had already written a play *The
Jews* (*Die Juden*, published in 1754) in which he deplored anti-Semitic
prejudice, but his friendship with Mendelssohn was his first close contact
with a Jew. As Lessing hoped, Mendelssohn's intellect and integrity were
recognized and he became an eminent philosopher, who believed that
the essential principles of his own religion could be reconciled with
modern enlightened secular learning. In *Nathan the Wise* Nathan is such
an enlightened Jew, and although the character, Nathan, is not a portrait
of Moses Mendelssohn, Mendelssohn probably had a considerable influ-
ence on Lessing's conception of the role.

The article *Philosophe* in the *Encyclopédie* (*Texts*, I p.9) speaks of:
'This love of society, which is so essential to the *philosophe*'. Lessing and
his friends were like the French *philosophes* in this respect. They had little
money, little time for frivolity, but meetings, clubs, long conversations
and discussions, and correspondence, were their life-blood.

---

[6]   Letter from Lessing to Friederich Nicolai, 25 August 1769 in document 45 in
Texts, I, Frederick the Great, King of Prussia, Letters and Documents, p.63.

[7]   See footnote 6.

[8]   Moses Mendelssohn was the grandfather of the composer Felix Mendelssohn-
Bartholdy.

[9]   To the Göttingen theologian and orientalist Johann David Michaelis.
(Lachmann-Muncker, Vol. XVII No.34).

Achievement and reputation

Lessing already had a considerable reputation as a writer when he was in his twenties. He had published poems, fables, literary criticism, studies in theological history, and five plays: *The Young Scholar, Damon, or True Friendship, The Old Maid, The Jews*, and *The Freethinker*. The plays were all comedies, but all had a moral content. Lessing's ideas about open-mindedness in religion and his criticism of prejudice and intolerance are clearly seen in *The Jews* and *The Freethinker*. In *The Jews* a baron is rescued from robbers by a stranger whom he welcomes to his home as a worthy and cultivated man. The baron, who has anti-Semitic prejudices, thinks that his attackers were Jews, but it turns out that they were his own servants in disguise, and that his rescuer is a noble-minded Jew.

In 1755 Lessing and Moses Mendelssohn collaborated on an essay: *Pope – a Metaphysician! (Pope – ein Metaphysiker!)*. The Berlin Academy of Sciences had offered a prize for an essay on Pope's proposition in the *Essay on Man* – 'whatever is, is right'. Their joint essay on this subject was scathing about any claim that Pope, as a poet, might have to a grasp of philosophy; but they were not critical of Leibniz, as Voltaire was shortly to be in his poem on the Lisbon disaster (1756) and *Candide* (1759). The Berlin Academy did not favour Leibniz's views. Lessing and Mendelssohn did not enter for the prize, but published their essay anonymously, well aware that they were dealing with a contentious issue of the Enlightenment.

The theory of drama was important too; it was not enough to formulate rules for drama, as Boileau[10] had done in seventeenth-century France, followed by Gottsched in Germany in 1730. The fundamental nature and purpose of drama had to be re-examined. Lessing, like so many of his enlightened contemporaries, had a deep respect for the Ancients. He had himself translated Plautus[11] and studied Aristotle's theory of drama. He shared this interest in drama with Nicolai and Mendelssohn, with both of whom he conducted a correspondence on tragedy, while Lessing's own articles on the drama appeared in a series of publications in the 1750s. The most important work was *Letters on Modern Literature*, which appeared in sections between 1759 and 1760. Diderot had said: 'Everything must be brought to light boldly, without exceptions, and unsparingly' (*Texts*, I, p.9). These three young men practised what Diderot preached. The articles on the theatre condemned adherence to French classical models, and praised Shakespeare and Lessing himself approved of the 'sentimental' comedy appearing in England and

---

[10] Boileau (Despreaux) Nicolas (1636–1711), French critic and poet and author of *L'Art poétique* (*The Art of Poetry*, 1674).

[11] Titus Maccius Plautus (*c.*254–184 BC) Roman writer of comic plays.

France.[12] In the same year Lessing published his translation of Diderot's plays in *The Theatre of Mr Diderot* (1760).

Practice had even more impact than theory. In 1755 Lessing had published his play *Miss Sara Sampson*, first produced in Frankfurt on the Oder with great success – the audience was in floods of tears at each performance. The play was much influenced by George Lillo's *The London Merchant; or, the History of George Barnwell* (1731) and by Richardson's novels. A tragedy about a seduced girl, in a contemporary everyday setting, was an affront to those who believed that all tragedy should be in high style and noble. 'A bourgeois tragedy! My God ... what is to become of us?' was Lessing's own ironic comment.[13]

About this time too Lessing had been studying Winckelmann's *Thoughts on the Imitation of Greek Works in Painting and Sculpture* (1755) and his *History of the Art of Antiquity* (1764). In 1755 he had translated du Bos's *Critical Reflections on Poetry and Painting.*[14] Lessing's own work on aesthetics was *Laoköon, or the Limits of Painting and Poetry*, in 1766, a work which came to be considered as one of the most important works on aesthetics in the eighteenth century. Winckelmann himself was impressed by Lessing's style of writing, though critical of his knowledge of the subject.

In the meantime there had been changes in Lessing's way of life. His one chance to go to England, in 1756, as travelling companion to a young businessman, Gottfried Winkler, was frustrated by the outbreak of the Seven Years' War. In 1760 he accepted the position of secretary to General Bogislaw Friedrich von Tauentzien, who was Prussian commandant in Breslau. Lessing wrote to his friends with no particular enthusiasm about the kind of life he led, but for a while his financial position improved. He could even indulge a little his love for gambling, which he could seldom afford, but in which he found excitement. Lessing fell seriously ill in Breslau and left his job before the end of the war. He had been proposed for the job of librarian in the Royal Library in Berlin, but Frederick, no doubt remembering Voltaire's complaints about Lessing, refused to consider him.

In his essay *On German Literature* (1780), Frederick the Great made no mention of Lessing and made only unfavourable general comments on German drama. Lessing's next work makes this omission even more striking. In 1767 appeared *Minna von Barnhelm*, a contemporary comedy, in which the action takes place at the end of the Seven Years' War. Goethe called it: 'The truest product of the Seven Years' War, the first

---

[12]   Eighteenth-century views of sentiment are discussed in the Introduction to Part E of the course.

[13]   26 April 1755 in the *Berlin Gazette.*

[14]   Abbé Jean-Baptiste du Bos (1670–1742) *Réflexions critiques sur la poésie et la peinture* (1719).

theatre production taken from real life, with a specific contemporary content'.[15] It was seen at the time, and can still be seen now, as the best modern comedy of the century in German. It was an instant success on the stage, first in Hamburg, then in Berlin. Lessing then took part in one of the most interesting experiments in the theatre of the time. A consortium of affluent citizens of the free city of Hamburg launched a 'national theatre'. Lessing was invited to become resident critic and adviser. He accepted. In this role he produced a work of lasting importance: *The Hamburg Dramaturgy* (1767). This is a collection of his reviews and commentaries. He soon had to give up writing about performances, as the actors were touchy about genuinely critical reviews, but the work continued as essays on the drama. The project failed. The directors quarrelled and there were financial problems. Lessing himself lost money heavily in a printing venture, had to sell his library, and consider what to do next.

He had made good friends in Hamburg, among them the son and daughter of Hermann Samuel Reimarus, philologist and orientalist, and a silk merchant. Engelbert König, and his wife, Eva. Englebert König died suddenly at the end of 1769, and Lessing had promised to look after his wife and children – a promise which he kept, although he had to leave Hamburg, as he had just accepted the position of Librarian at Wolfenbüttel.

Wolfenbüttel – controversial Librarian

In accepting the post of Librarian in the great library of the Duke of Brunswick in Wolfenbüttel, Lessing was giving in at last and accepting patronage. As a scholar he found the work rewarding and discovered some valuable manuscripts, (including an eleventh-century manuscript of Berengar de Tours, the discovery of which made an important contribution to church history). Yet he was lonely, isolated in a gloomy, empty castle, since the Duke's court had moved to Brunswick. He had a secure position, but he was still poor, even though he was now eminent as a writer. *Minna von Barnhelm* was being performed with great success, and his new play, a tragedy, *Emilia Galotti*, was first performed in Brunswick in 1772, and highly praised.

For Lessing personal plans became most important. Slowly his friendship with Eva König became love, and they decided to marry; but Eva, who was a woman of courage, charm and intelligence, had had to take over her late husband's business affairs, which involved lengthy journeys and long stays in Vienna. Over the years it was a friendship, then courtship by correspondence, with rare meetings. Eventually, Lessing managed to secure from the Duke of Brunswick a higher salary and a

---

[15]   Goethe, *Dichtung und Wahrheit* (*Poetry and Truth*), Part II Book 7.

house in Wolfenbüttel. They married in 1776. For one year of his life Lessing was perfectly happy; but at the end of the year Eva had a child who died, and shortly afterwards she too died. Lessing found only one way to cope with his personal tragedy, and that was to work, and work meant fighting – and fighting about fundamental religious issues which had concerned him all his life.

A few months after his wife's death, Lessing became involved in a very bitter and very public controversy. It came to a head in 1778, although it had started some years before. Publication of really controversial views on religion was still hazardous. One notable man with radical views was Professor Reimarus (1694–1768) of Hamburg, the father of Lessing's two friends. He had written an *Apologia or Plea for the Rational Worshippers of God* (*Apologie oder Schutzschrift für die vernünftigen Verehrer Gottes*, 1778). He did not venture to publish it in his lifetime. Lessing had acquired the manuscript (and was carefully evasive about how he had done so) and used his right as Wolfenbüttel Librarian to publish extracts as *Fragments of an Anonymous Author* in 1774 and 1777. Hostile comments came from critics of modest standing, to which Lessing's most notable reply was the essay *'eine Duplik'* (*'A Rejoinder'*); but then more imposing critics joined in. Lessing's main opponent was Johann Melchior Goeze (1717–86), Chief Pastor of the Katherinenkirche in Hamburg, an orthodox Lutheran theologian and scholar. For some months in 1778 the battle was conducted, through a series of pamphlets, about criticism of revealed religion and the right to express such views. Lessing's opponents succeeded in persuading the Duke of Brunswick to withdraw the Librarian's right to publish papers, and Lessing was forbidden to publish anything more on religion. His response was to put his ideas into the play *Nathan the Wise*, which made a strong case for the unprejudiced pursuit of religious truth and for toleration.[16]

In 1778 Lessing had published the first part of his *Gespräche für Freymäurer* (*Ernst and Falk: Dialogues on Freemasonry*), and in 1780 he published *The Education of the Human Race* (*Die Erziehung des Menschengeschlechts*). By then he was exhausted and ill, and wrote no more major works. He died in Brunswick in 1781.

Chronological outline of Lessing's life and main works

1729   born 22 January in Kamenz, Saxony.

1741–6   At St Afra electoral school in Meissen.

1746–8   Student at University of Leipzig.

1748   *The Young Scholar* performed by the Neuber company.

---

[16] There is a detailed discussion of the religious controversy in Lessing and Religion in *Religion and Humanity: Lessing's Nathan the Wise* (*Studies*, II).

1748	In Wittenberg. At the end of the year goes to Berlin.
1749	Writes *The Jews*.
1750	Journalist for the *Berlin Gazette* with his cousin Johann Christlob Mylius.
1751	Translation of Voltaire's *Minor Historical Works*.
1752	In Wittenberg obtains Master's degree.
1753–5	Publication of collected works in six volumes.
1753	Translates Marigny's *History of the Arabs*.
1754	*The Jews* and *The Young Scholar* published.
1754	Meets Friedrich Nicolai and Moses Mendelssohn.
1755	*Pope – a Metaphysician!* written with Mendelssohn.
1755	The *Freethinker* published.
1755	Translation of du Bos's *Critical Reflections on Poetry and Painting*.
1755	*Miss Sara Sampson* performed and published.
1756	Journey to England interrupted by the Seven Years' War.
1757	In Leipzig.
1758–60	In Berlin.
1759	*Letters on Modern Literature*.
1759	*Philotas* – a tragedy.
	Fables
1760	*The Theatre of Mr Diderot*.
1760–5	In Breslau as secretary to General von Tauentzien.
1764	Serious illness in Breslau.
1765–7	In Berlin.
1766	*Laoköon or the Limits of Painting and Poetry*.
1767	*Minna von Barnhelm*.
1767–70	In Hamburg as critic and adviser for the Hamburg theatre.
1767	*Hamburg Dramaturgy*.
1769	*Antiquarian Letters*.
	The Ancients' View of Death.
	Friendship with the Reimarus and König families.
1770	Librarian of the ducal library in Wolfenbüttel.
1771	Engagement to Eva König.
1772	*Emilia Galotti*.

1774   Publishes first *Fragments of an Anonymous Author.*
1775   Journey to Leipzig, Dresden, Vienna.
        Journey to Italy with Prince Leopold of Brunswick.
1776   Marriage to Eva König.
1777   Journey to Mannheim. Refuses offer to direct Mannheim theatre.
1778   Death of his wife Eva.
1778   Dispute with Chief Pastor Goeze. *Anti-Goeze* pamphlets.
1778   *Ernst and Falk* – dialogues for freemasons.
1779   *Nathan the Wise.*
1780   *The Education of the Human Race.*
1781   15 February, died in Brunswick.

Nathan the Wise

The setting of the play

The scene of the play is given as Jerusalem. The action takes place during an armistice in the Crusades. The year therefore must be 1192 at the end of the Third Crusade which lasted from 1189 to 1192. There are references in the play to Richard I (Coeur de Lion) and Philippe August II of France who were both in Palestine in 1191, and to Emperor Frederick I Barbarossa, who also took part in the Crusade and was drowned in Armenia in 1190.

The Crusades were military expeditions, fostered by the Papacy, undertaken from the eleventh to the thirteenth centuries by European Christians. The aim was to gain the Christian holy places in Palestine, then under Muslim occupation. After some successful military operations the Kingdom of Jerusalem was established and had then to be defended. In 1187 Sultan Saladin recaptured Jerusalem. The aim of the Third Crusade, led by the English and French kings and the German emperor, was to regain Jerusalem. The Europeans did not succeed in doing this, but Saladin made a treaty with Richard I, in effect an agreement to a three year armistice, which included permission for unarmed Christians to visit the holy places in Jerusalem.

Lessing's main historical source was François Louis Claude Marin's (1721–1809) *History of Saladin Sultan of Egypt and Syria,* (*Histoire de Saladin. Sulthan d'Egypte et de Syrie,* Paris 1758), translated into German by E.G. Küster, 1761. Lessing had himself translated Voltaire's *History of the*

Crusades in 1751 and Abbé de Marigny's *History of the Arabs* in 1753 (*Histoire des Arabes sous le Gouvernement des Califes*, Paris, 1750). Lessing did not set out to write a historical play. He was not concerned with historical accuracy, although such details as he gives broadly fit in with the historical facts, except for some points of chronology: for example, Saladin's father, who is mentioned, was no longer alive in 1192, and it is implied in the play that Frederick Barbarossa had died many years before. There is also a quite deliberate anachronistic reference to the theatre.

Lessing's main concern was to present his parable in circumstances where Christians, Jews and Muslims could plausibly be in communication. He had made an uncompromising comment on the Crusades in the *Hamburg Dramaturgy* (Part 7): 'These Crusades, which in their inception had been a political stratagem of the Popes, in practice led to the most inhuman persecutions of which Christian superstition has ever been guilty.'

The characters

Sultan Saladin The historical Salah-el-Din lived from 1138 to 1193. He was a Kurd who first gained power in Egypt, then waged successful campaigns in Syria and Mesopotamia, and conquered Jerusalem in 1187. Saladin made a treaty with Richard I in 1192 (see above). The plan, mentioned in the play, to marry Richard's sister Johanna to Saladin's brother Melek seems to have some foundation in fact.

Sittah Saladin had a sister called Sitt-alscham (also Sillah-Alscham in Marin's history). This suggested the name to Lessing.

Nathan Lessing based the scenes with the parable of the three rings on a story in Boccaccio's *Decamaron* in which a Jew named Melchisedech plays the main part. Lessing chose instead the name Nathan, an Old Testament prophet, for his principal character, as a more suitable name to use for his verse drama.

Recha was called Rahel in Lessing's first draft of the play.

Daja 'As I understand it, Daja means something like Nutrix (nurse)' Lessing noted in his draft of the play.

A young Templar The order of Knights Templar was founded in 1118, to protect pilgrims to the Holy Land. The name came from the fact that the order's base was near to what was held to be Solomon's temple in Jerusalem. The Templars took vows of poverty, chastity and obedience. Their uniform was a white cloak with a octagonal red cross on the breast.

A Dervish A Muhammadan mendicant monk.

The Patriarch of Jerusalem The bishop of Jerusalem. From the fifth century the bishops of Rome, Alexandria, Antioch, Byzantium and Jerusalem were given the rank of Patriarch. The Patriarch at the time of the Third Crusade was Heraklius, an infamous character according to Marin's *History of Saladin*.

A *Lay Brother* Lay brothers were not ordained, took only a vow of obedience, and carried out humbler tasks in monasteries.

An Emir An independent Muslim ruler.

Mamelukes Members of the Sultan's bodyguard.

The verse form and translation

Lessing chose to use blank verse, that is unrhymed iambic pentameters. Up to this time blank verse had been rarely used in German, but soon, in the plays of Goethe and Schiller and other dramatists, it became the verse form most often used in German drama.

Lessing was a master of vigorous, incisive prose and of dramatic language. His use of the verse in *Nathan the Wise* seems almost casual: it is clearly subordinated to the needs of the drama. It uses everyday, even colloquial language, appropriate to the different characters: the direct and simple language of the Lay Brother, the Patriarch's pious clichés, the sometimes 'romantic' language of the Templar, the changing styles of Nathan himself in different contexts. Lessing's friends pointed to much that was 'incorrect' in the early drafts, such as many lines with six or four feet instead of five. Lessing eliminated some of these, but gave priority to meaning and dramatic effect. Frequent *enjambements*[17] are necessary, for the sake of the dialogue; in long sentences over many lines predicate and subject may be separated, pronouns or adverbs may not be used in the same line as the words with which they are associated. But Lessing had his own good reasons for this use of language, and remained in control. A more obviously 'poetic' feature in the play is its imagery, the recurring images of fire and water, trees and flowers – images intended to stimulate ideas and establish connections in the mind of the reader. There are biblical references or allusions, possibly more familiar to Lessing's contemporaries than to present-day readers. In the play as a whole, the flexibility of the verse, even its uneven rhythms, contribute to the intensity of its forward-moving ideas.

Inevitably much is lost in translation. The translation conveys Lessing's meaning as faithfully as possible, in a verse form which has some correspondence with Lessing's own. Complex German constructions have been simplified where this does not distort the meaning; the play on words in which Lessing delighted emerges in somewhat muted form; his juxtapositions and play on the sound of words tend to get lost, and epigrammatic phrases lose force. But the play's pace, concentrated flow of ideas, its fairly colloquial style, its general informality and humour perhaps emerge.

---

[17] enjambement – in verse, the carrying on of the sense of a line or couplet into the next.

Publication and performance

Lessing wrote *Nathan the Wise* in 1779. He arranged for it to be published and sold on subscription. Editions were then produced and sold by the publisher Voss.

There were no performances in Lessing's lifetime. The first performance was given in Berlin in 1783 by the company run by a well-known actor-manager, Döbbelin, who played the part of Nathan.

It was performed in Lübeck in 1788 and in Hamburg in 1789, and later established a place in the theatre repertoire.

Nathan the Wise was first translated into French in 1783 and into English by William Taylor of Norwich in 1790 (privately printed, and later issued for sale in 1805).

Title and epigraph

Lessing called *Nathan the Wise* 'a dramatic poem'. Voltaire had used this description for his play *The Ghebers or Tolerance* (*Les Guèbres ou la tolérance*) in 1769. Despite Lessing's criticism of Voltaire there are features of *Nathan the Wise* which have something in common with the theme of this play and others by Voltaire, *Zaire* (1732) and *Mahomet* (1742).

On the title page appears the epigraph:

Introite, nam et heic Dii sunt!

APUD GELLIUM

Enter, for here too are gods

From the works of Gellius

The reference is to the preface to *Noctes Atticae* (Attic or Athenian Nights) of Aulus Gellius,who lived c.AD 130–175.

References

Aner, K. (1929) *The Theology of the Age of Lessing* (*Die Theologie der Lessingzeit*), Halle.

Garland, H. B. (1962) *Lessing The Founder of Modern German Literature*, 2nd edn., London.

Nathan the Wise

A dramatic poem in five acts

Introite, nam et heic Dii sunt!
  Apud Gellium
by
Gotthold Ephraim Lessing
1779

Dramatis Personae

Sultan Saladin
Sittah, his sister
Nathan, a rich Jew in Jerusalem
Recha, his adopted daughter
Daja, a Christian but living in the house of the Jew, as Recha's companion
A young Templar
A Dervish
The Patriarch of Jerusalem
A Lay Brother
An Emir
and Mamelukes of Saladin

The scene is Jerusalem at the end of the twelfth century.

[**Note**. The lines have been numbered to correspond with those of the German text. In a few cases where the English translation is shorter, an adjustment has been made, and this is indicated against the lines in question.]

Gotthold Ephraim Lessing
Nathan the Wise

Act I

Scene 1
Nathan and Daja

(Scene: A hall in Nathan's house. Nathan comes in from his journey. Daja meets him.)

DAJA	He's here! It's Nathan! God be praised That you have come back home at last.	
NATHAN	Yes, Daja, God be praised. But why *at last?* Did I intend to come home any sooner? Could I if I'd wished to? Babylon Is from Jerusalem at least two hundred miles Away along the route I was Obliged to take, with detours right and left. Collecting in of debts is not a job That makes a journey shorter, not something That is rushed, or quickly set aside.	5 10
DAJA	Oh Nathan, When I think how wretched you'd have been If you had stayed at home. Your house ...	
NATHAN	Was burnt. Yes, that I have already learned – God grant That they have really told me everything.	15
DAJA	And it was nearly totally destroyed.	
NATHAN	Then, Daja, we'd have simply built ourselves Another – and a better one.	
DAJA	That's true. Yet Recha was so very nearly burnt To death.	
NATHAN	My Recha, burnt to death? My Recha? I had not heard that. Well then I would not Have needed any house. So she was nearly Burnt to death! You mean it's really true? She's burnt to death! Just tell me now straight out! Admit it! – kill me: torture me no longer. – Yes, she's burnt to death!	20 25

DAJA   If that were so
Would you be hearing it from me?

NATHAN   Why do you terrify me then? – O Recha
O, my Recha.

DAJA   Yours? Your Recha?

NATHAN   If ever I no longer were allowed   30
To call this child my own!

DAJA   Can you call everything
That you possess with equal right
Your own?

NATHAN   Nothing with greater right. All else
That I possess has been bestowed on me
By nature or good fortune. This alone   35
I owe to virtue.

DAJA   Nathan, what a price
You make me pay for all your kindness.
If kindness carried out with such intent
Can still deserve that name.

NATHAN   With such intent?
With what intent?

DAJA   My conscience ...

NATHAN   Daja, first   40
Of all, just let me tell you what I bought ...

DAJA   I can't ignore my conscience ...

NATHAN   What lovely cloth
I bought for you in Babylon. So rich
And yet so elegant as well. Recha
Herself will scarce have any finer.

DAJA   It's   45
No use. For my conscience I must tell you,
Will not be silenced for much longer now.

NATHAN   I wonder how you'll like the bracelets, earrings
Necklace and the ring which I selected
Just for you when I was in Damascus.   50
I really long to know.

DAJA   That's so like you!
Only content if you can give and give!

NATHAN   Take gladly, as I give – and say no more!

DAJA   No more! Who questions, Nathan, that there's none
More honest and more generous than you.   55
And yet! ...

NATHAN	And yet I'm just a Jew – Is that What you want to say!
DAJA	You know much better What I want to say.
NATHAN	Well then be quiet!
DAJA	Very well. What happens here, that's unacceptable To God I can neither alter nor prevent. 60 So – be it on your head![18]
NATHAN	Yes, be it on my head! But where is she then? Just tell me! – Daja, Are you deceiving me? Does she not know That I have come back home?
DAJA	How can you ask? Still terror shakes her, every nerve in her, 65 In her fantasy she still imagines fire In all she sees. Her mind's awake when she's asleep, And sleeps when she's awake – now lower Than the beasts, now higher than the angels.
NATHAN	Poor child! That's only human.
DAJA	This morning 70 She lay so long with tight shut eyes and was As dead. Then started up and cried out 'listen'! 'My father's camels are arriving home'! 'Listen, I hear his gentle voice'! And then Her eyes grew dim and then her head, which now 75 Was not supported by her arm, fell back Onto the pillow. I went to the gate! And saw you there. You really had come home. Can you wonder at it? Her entire soul Was all this time with you – and him –
NATHAN	Him? 80 Who is he?
DAJA	The man who rescued her From the fire.
NATHAN	Who was he? Who? – Where is he? Who saved my Recha for me, who was it?

---

[18]   Matthew 27:25. 'Then answered all the people and said. His blood be on us and on our children.'

DAJA	A young Knight Templar who, not many days
	Ago was brought here as a captive, then 85
	Was pardoned by the Sultan Saladin.
NATHAN	What? Saladin has spared a Templar's life?
	A *Templar's life?*. Only such a miracle
	Could save my Recha? Oh God!
DAJA	Without
	This man who boldly risked his life again 90
	Which he had just regained, she would have died.
NATHAN	Where is he, Daja, where's this noble man?
	Where is he? Let me go and kneel to him.
	I hope you gave him first of all, those treasures
	Which I left you? Gave him everything? 95
	And promised more, much more?
DAJA	How could we?
NATHAN	You did not?
DAJA	He came, no one knows from where,
	He went, and no one knows where to – without
	A knowledge of the house, and guided just
	By what he heard, he rushed with cloak outspread 100
	Boldly through flame and smoke to reach the voice
	Of someone crying 'Help!' By then we thought
	He must be lost – But from the smoke and flame
	He suddenly appeared. In his strong arms
	He held her safe. Coldly and quite unmoved 105
	By all our praise and thanks, he set her down,
	Forced his way through the crowd who waited there –
	And disappeared.
NATHAN	Not for ever, I should hope.
DAJA	Afterwards for several days we saw
	Him walking up and down beneath the palms 110
	Which shade the Holy Sepulchre.[19]
	I went up to him with rapture, thanked him.
	Praised him, implored, besought him just once more
	To see the gentle pious girl who
	Cannot now find rest, until she's thanked him 115
	With many tears, kneeling at his feet.
NATHAN	And then?
DAJA	In vain! Deaf to our request
	He poured such bitter scorn on me especially ...

---

[19] The grave of the resurrected Christ.

NATHAN	That you were frightened off?

DAJA   Quite the contrary!
Every day I went to him again   120
And every day again he taunted me.
How much I bore from him! Much more I would
Have gladly borne! But for a long time now
He has not come to walk beneath the palms
Which cast their shade upon the Holy Sepulchre.   125
And no one knows where he has gone.
You're amazed? and thoughtful?

NATHAN   I was thinking
What impression on a mind like Recha's
This must surely have. To find herself
Disdained by one whom she feels bound to   130
Esteem; to be rejected and yet so
Attracted by him. Truly heart and head
Must long have argued whether bitterness
Or sorrow now should dominate.
Often neither wins; and fantasy   135
Which joins the conflict too, makes dreamers.
Sometimes their head may rule their heart, sometimes
Again their heart may rule their head – a choice
Of evils! – If I know her well, this must
Be Recha's case: she dreams.

DAJA   But so devout.   140
So lovable!

NATHAN   A dreamer none the less!

DAJA   She has one dream – a fancy, if you like,
Most dear to her. It's that her Templar is
No mortal man, no son of mortal man,
But one of the angels, whom her young heart   145
From childhood onwards loved to think of as
Her own protector. Stepping from the cloud
Which veiled him, hovering round her even in
The fire, he suddenly appeared in Templar's
Form – don't smile at her! – Who knows? or if   150
You smile, let her at least emjoy a dream
Where Christian, Jew and Muslim can unite
As one – a dream that is so sweet!

NATHAN   Sweet
To me as well! – go, honest Daja, go
See what she's doing – whether I can speak   155
To her. And then I'll find this wild capricious
Guardian angel. If it pleases him

	To dwell with us below a little while,	
	Playing at chivalry with such ill grace,	
	I'll surely find him out and bring him here.	160
DAJA	It won't be easy. Nathan.	
NATHAN	Then perhaps	
	The sweet dream will give way to sweeter truth –	
	Believe me, Daja, to a human being	
	A human is much dearer than an angel.	
	So you will not blame me too much, I hope,	165
	When you shall see our angel-dreamer cured.	
DAJA	You are so good, and yet you are so bad!	
	I'll go. But – listen! – look! – she's coming here herself.	

Scene 2

Recha, Nathan and Daja

RECHA	Father! So it *is* you, safe and sound.	
	I thought it might be just your voice, sent on	170
	Ahead. Why have you stopped out here? What hills,	
	What deserts and what streams divide us now?	
	You're breathing in a room just next to mine	
	Instead of rushing to embrace your Recha –	
	Poor Recha who was meanwhile burnt to death!	175
	Or nearly burnt, just nearly. So don't shudder!	
	It is a dreadful death, to burn.	
NATHAN	My child, my dearest child!	
RECHA	•You must have crossed	
	Euphrates, Tigris, Jordan: and who knows	
	How many other rivers? – Often I	180
	Have trembled for you, until the fire came	
	So near to me. But since the fire has come	
	So near to me: to die in water seems	
	Refreshment, comfort, and deliverance.	
	And yet you are not drowned, and I have not	185
	Been burnt to death. Let us now rejoice	
	And praise our God. He surely bore you and	
	Your boat on wings of his unseen angels ·	
	Across the treacherous streams. And it was God	
	Who beckoned to my angel to be seen,	190
	Carrying me through the flames on his white wings.	
NATHAN	(On his white wings – of course!, That must have been	
	The Templar's white and outspread cloak)[20]	

---

[20] The Templar's uniform was a white cloak with an octagonal red cross on the left breast.

RECHA   Visibly, *visibly*
                    He bore me through the fire, protected by
                    His wings. And so I saw an angel, and   195
                    I saw him face to face; He was my *own*
                    Angel.

NATHAN   Worthy of my Recha. And
                    There's nothing fairer she would see in him
                    Than he in her.

RECHA   *(smiling)*
                                  Whom do you flatter, father,
                    The angel, or yourself?

NATHAN   Yet if he were   200
                    A human – such as nature shows us every day,
                    Who rendered you this service, he would seem
                    To you an angel. He must and so he would.

RECHA   Not that kind of angel, no! A real one:
                    He was, I'm sure, a real one! Haven't you   205
                    Taught me yourself that angels really could
                    Exist, and miracles are worked by God
                    To benefit all those who love him truly?
                    I do love him.

NATHAN   Yes, and he loves you
                    And hourly he works miracles for you   210
                    And those like you. So has he done for all
                    Eternity.

RECHA   That makes me happy.

NATHAN   Why?
                    It might sound natural and commonplace
                    If he who saved you were a real Templar
                    Knight; but surely that would be no less a   215
                    Miracle! – The greatest miracle
                    Is that those miracles which are both real and true
                    Can and do become so commonplace to us.
                    Without this universal miracle
                    No thinking person would call miracles   220
                    Those things which only seem so to a child,
                    Who stares at and pursues the strangest things,
                    Struck only by their novelty.

DAJA *(TO
NATHAN)*   Are you
                    Intending to destroy her mind, already
                    So inflamed, with all this subtlety?   225

NATHAN   Patience! For my Recha isn't it a
                    Miracle enough that she was rescued

By a human being who himself was earlier
Saved by no small miracle. Indeed
A miracle! Whoever heard of any   230
Templar Knight reprieved by Saladin?
Or any Templar who has asked or hoped
That he would spare him? Or who offered more
To him for freedom than the leather belt[21]
Which holds his sword, or at most his dagger?   235

RECHA   Father that proves my point, that he was not
A Templar Knight. He merely looked like one –
No Templar who was captured ever comes
Into Jerusalem except to certain death;
No Templar walks so freely in Jerusalem: 240
How could any Templar have been free
To save me in the dark?

NATHAN   Why, that's well argued,
Now, Daja, tell us. For it was from you
That I have heard that he was sent here as
A prisoner. I'm sure you must know more.   245

DAJA   Well yes – that's what they say – but they
Also say that Saladin has pardoned
Him because he looks so like one of
His brothers, one whom he loved dearly.
But as it's more than twenty years ago now   250
Since this brother was alive – and I don't
Know his name – and don't know where he died,
It all just sounds so – so incredible,
I dare say that there's nothing in it.

NATHAN   Daja, Why should such a thing be so   255
Incredible? Surely not because
You've chosen to believe in something *more*
Incredible, as others do? Saladin
Loves all his family. He might indeed
Have loved one of his brothers in particular   260
When he was young. And you'll agree it's true
Two faces often look alike – are
Impressions lost because they're old? And doesn't
The same cause produce the same effect?
It must. What is incredible in this?   265
But I suppose, wise Daja, that you'd not

---

[21]   The belt in fact was of linen not leather, but if a Templar gave up his belt, he renounced his adherence to the order.

Consider that a miracle – your miracles
Need faith – or rather, should I say, deserve it.

DAJA   You're mocking me.

NATHAN   Because you're mocking *me*.
But even so, Recha, you're rescue *was*   270
A miracle, achieved by him who guides,
With slenderest of threads, the firm resolves,
The boldest plans of kings, as if it were
His sport, if not his mockery.

RECHA   Father!
If I'm wrong, you know I'm wrong against   275
My will.

NATHAN   I know you're eager to be taught.
Look! A forehead with a certain arch,
A nose whose bridge is shaped in one way rather
Than another, eyebrows curving in
A particular way along a broad or narrow   280
Ridge of bone – a line, a mark, a curve
A fold, an angle, insignificant details
On a wild European's face –
And you escape the burning fire in Asia.
If you're hungering for miracles,   285
That *is* a miracle. Why conjure up
An angel too?

DAJA   But Nathan, if you'll let me speak,
What's the harm in thinking you've been rescued
By an angel rather than a human
Being? Can't it make you feel much closer   290
To the mysterious first cause of your rescue?

NATHAN   Pride! Nothing but pride! The iron pot
Wants to be lifted from the fire with silver
Tongs, in order to imagine it's a pot
Of silver. Ha! What folly! Where's the harm   295
In that, you ask me, Where's the harm in it?
What's the use of it, I might reply.
For your 'Feeling so much nearer to God'
Is either nonsense or else blasphemy.
And there *is* harm in it, there really is.   300
Now listen. Is it true that both of you,
But Recha above all, want to repay
Your rescuer, whether he's an angel or
A human being, by doing some great service?
You do? Well, to an angel, what service,   305
What great service could you hope to give?

	You might give thanks, and sigh and pray to him;	
	You might dissolve in tears of ecstasy;	
	You might celebrate his festivals	
	By fasting, or give alms – but all that's nothing.	310
	It strikes me that your dear ones and yourselves	
	Gain far more by all this than he. He won't	
	Get fat from all your fasting, or get rich	
	From your donations; he won't gain in splendour	
	From your ecstasy, he won't be mightier	315
	By your faith. But if he were a man!	
DAJA	Yes, if he were a man there would be greater	
	Opportunity to *do* something.	
	And God knows, we were eager to serve him.	
	But he wanted nothing, needed nothing	320
	From us; in himself, and with himself	
	He was content, as angels are, and only	
	Angels can be.	
RECHA	When at last he vanished …	
NATHAN	Vanished? – Really vanished? – You no longer	
	Saw him walk beneath the palms? But have	325
	You really made a thorough search for him?	
DAJA	Well, no, we haven't.	
NATHAN	How's that possible?	
	What's the harm, you say – you cruel dreamers! –	
	Suppose this angel now – had fallen ill?	
RECHA	Ill?	
DAJA	Ill! He's surely not!	
RECHA	A cold chill makes	330
	Me shudder. Daja! feel my face. It was	
	So warm and now it's just like ice.	
NATHAN	He's	
	A Frank,[22] who's unaccustomed to our climate.	
	He's young, not hardened to the rigours of	
	His order, to the hunger, sleeplessness.	335
RECHA	Ill!	
DAJA	Nathan only means he might be.	
NATHAN	Lying there, with neither friends nor gold	
	To buy himself some friends.	
RECHA	Oh father, no!	

---

[22] Since the first Crusade (1096–99), which started in France, Frank was used in the Middle East to denote all European Christians.

NATHAN	He lies bereft of nursing, sympathy,	
	Or help, a prey to suffering and death!	340
RECHA	Where? Where?	
NATHAN	For someone he had never known	
	Or seen – simply for a human being,	
	He rushed into the fire ...	
DAJA	Nathan, spare her!	
NATHAN	He did not want to know the one he'd saved,	
	Nor see her any more, he only wanted	345
	To avoid her thanks ...	
DAJA	Spare her, Nathan!	
NATHAN	He had no wish to see her any more – unless	
	He had to rescue her a second time	
	Enough, it was a human being ...	
DAJA	Stop!	
NATHAN	His only consolation as he dies	350
	Is his awareness of this deed!	
DAJA	Stop!	
	You're killing her!	
NATHAN	And you have killed him! – or	
	You could have done so. – Recha, Recha, I am	
	Offering you medicine not poison.	
	He's alive – calm down! – he's probably not ill;	355
	Not even ill.	
RECHA	Really? Not dead? Not ill?	
NATHAN	Really, He's not dead! For God rewards us	
	In this world for doing good. Now,	
	See, how rapturous dreaming is much easier	
	Than doing good. The weakest people like	360
	To indulge in pious rapture – even though	
	They're often unaware of why they do it –	
	Simply to avoid the work of doing	
	Good.	
RECHA	Father, don't ever leave your Recha	
	On her own again – You think perhaps	365
	He's only gone away?	
NATHAN	Yes, yes, – Of course –	
	But I can see a Muslim with enquiring	
	Eyes examining my laden camels.	
	Do you know who he is?	
DAJA	Ah! your dervish.	
NATHAN	Who?	

DAJA	Your dervish. Your old chess companion.	370
NATHAN	Al-Hafi? That's Al-Hafi?	
DAJA	He's become The Sultan's Treasurer.	
NATHAN	Is this a dream Again? It is Al-Hafi, coming here! Quick, go in. What has he got to say?	

Scene 3

Nathan and the Dervish

DERVISH	Open your eyes, as wide as they can go!	375
NATHAN	Is it you? Or isn't it? – In such fine clothes, A dervish!	
DERVISH	Well? Why not then? Do you think A dervish can't make something of himself?	
NATHAN	Well, yes, of course, – But I was thinking that A dervish – that's a real dervish – chooses To make nothing of himself.	380
DERVISH	By the Prophet,[23] It may well be that I am no real dervish, But if one must –	
NATHAN	Must! Dervish! – A dervish must? No-one must must,[24] and a dervish must. What must he then?	
DERVISH	What he is rightly asked to do And knows is good – that's what a dervish must.	385
NATHAN	By our God! You speak the truth – Let me Embrace you, man – I hope you're still my friend?	
DERVISH	And you don't ask first what I have become?	
NATHAN	In spite of that!	
DERVISH	But what if I'd become A state official in fine robes, one whose Friendship could be awkward?	390
NATHAN	If your heart Is still a dervish's, I'll take the risk. The state official's robes are just your dress.	

---

[23] i.e. by Mohammed! – equivalent of by God!

[24] 'Kein Mensch muss müssen' in the German text.

DERVISH	But even that commands respect. What do	395
	You think? What would I be at *your* court?	
NATHAN	Just	

DERVISH   But even that commands respect. What do   395

DERVISH	Me?
	Not much. But you could make a handsome profit. 425
	When the treasure's at its lowest ebb –
	You open up your floodgates – make advances,
	And claim any rate of interest.
NATHAN	And interest on the interest too?
DERVISH	Of course.
NATHAN	Until my capital is nothing more 430
	Than interest.
DERVISH	It doesn't tempt you? Then
	You'd better write a farewell letter to
	Our friendship. I was really counting on you.
NATHAN	Really? How?
DERVISH	I thought that you might help me
	Carry out my office with some honour. 435
	That I could use you as a source of funds –
	You shake your head?
NATHAN	Let's understand each other.
	A distinction must be made. For you, Al-Hafi,
	Why not? I'm always ready to do anything
	To help my friend the dervish. But 440
	Al-Hafi, treasurer to Saladin,
	To such a man ...
DERVISH	I thought as much. You're still
	As good as you are shrewd, and as shrewd
	As you are wise! Be patient. Soon the two
	Al-Hafis you distinguish will be separate 445
	Again. Look at this robe from Saladin
	Before it's worn out, and reduced to rags,
	Which are the proper clothing of a dervish,
	I'll hang it on a peg here in Jerusalem,
	And go off to the Ganges[25] where, with light 450
	And naked feet, I'll tread the hot sands with
	My teachers.
NATHAN	Just like you!
DERVISH	And I'll play chess
	With them.
NATHAN	Your highest bliss!
DERVISH	What tempted me –
	The prospect that my begging days were over?

---

[25] The holy river of the Hindus.

	A chance to play the rich man to the beggars?	455
	The ability to transform in a flash
	The richest beggar to a poor rich man?

NATHAN   Not that, I'm sure.

DERVISH   No, even more banal;
The new experience of being flattered;
Flattered by the Sultan's generous caprice.   460

NATHAN   Which was?

DERVISH   'Only a beggar knows how beggars
Feel; only a beggar knows, from his
Experience, just how to give to beggars.
Your predecessor was too cold', he said,
'Too harsh. He was so grudging when he gave: 465
He asked so many awkward questions first
About the recipient. Although he knew
There was a need, he wasn't satisfied
Unless he knew the *cause* of need. And so
The gift was meanly balanced with the cause.   470
Al-Hafi won't do that. And Saladin
With Hafi's help won't seem so niggardly.
Al-Hafi won't be like those blocked-up water pipes
Which spew out frothing and unclean
The water which came in so clear and still.   475
Al-Hafi thinks, Al-Hafi feels as I do!"
So sweetly trilled the fowler's pipe until
The bird was in the net! – Oh what a fool
I am! A fool of fools!

NATHAN   Gently, my dervish.
Gently!

DERVISH   Isn't it plain folly, when   480
A hundred thousand people are oppressed,
Impoverished, despoiled, tortured, slaughtered,
To play philanthropist to individuals?
Isn't it foolishness to simulate
The Almighty's mercy, which he casts impartially   485
On good and bad, on field and desert, both
In sunshine and in rain – to simulate it,
But without the hand of the Almighty
Which is always full. Don't tell me that's
Not folly.

NATHAN   That's enough, Al-Hafi!

DERVISH   And   490
My folly. Just consider that! Isn't
It folly to detect a trace of goodness

	In this foolishness, and just because	
	Of one good element, to take a part	
	In all this foolishness myself? Well?	495
	Isn't that the truth?	
NATHAN	Al-Hafi – you must	
	Go back to your desert. If you stay	
	Among the human race you might forget	
	To be a human.	
DERVISH	That's what I fear.	
	Farewell.	
NATHAN	But why are you in such a hurry?	500
	Wait, Al-Hafi! Will your desert run	
	Away? If he'd just listen! – Hey, Al-Hafi, stop! –	
	He's gone; I really should have liked to ask	
	Him all about our Templar. I imagine	
	He must know him.	

Scene 4

Daja and Nathan

DAJA	*(hurrying in)*	
	Nathan, Nathan!	
NATHAN	Well?	
	What is it now?	
DAJA	He has appeared again! He has	
	Appeared again!	
NATHAN	Who, Daja? Who?	
DAJA	He! He!	
NATHAN	He? He? – When hasn't He appeared![26] – Ah yes,	
	For you, there's just one He. – He shouldn't be!	
	Not even if he were an angel!	510
DAJA	He's strolling up and down under the	
	Palms; and he picks dates from time to time.	
NATHAN	And eats them too? – as if he were a Templar?	
DAJA	Why tease me? – Recha's eager eyes caught sight	
	Of him between the dense rows of the palms	515
	And followed him intently – now she asks you –	
	Pleads with you – to go and see him right away.	
	Hurry! She'll signal from the window	
	If he's coming up this way or turning	
	Back. Please hurry!	

---

[26] For Nathan 'He' means God.

NATHAN	Just as I've dismounted	520
	From my camel? – Would that be proper? *You* go	
	Quickly to him; tell him I've returned.	
	It was only in my absence that	
	The gentleman would not come to my house.	
	He'll gladly come when Recha's father sends	525
	An invitation. Go, and say that I	
	Request him, cordially ...	
DAJA	No use! He won't	
	Come to you – in short; he won't come to a Jew.	
NATHAN	Well go in any case; at least detain him;	
	Or failing that, just use your eyes to follow	530
	Him. Now go, and I'll come after you.	

(Nathan goes quickly indoors and Daja goes out)

Scene 5

Templar and Lay Brother
> *Scene: An open space with palm trees, under which the Templar is walking up and down.*
> *A Lay Brother is following him at some distance at the side looking as if he wants to speak to him.*

TEMPLAR	He can't be following me for nothing!
	See how he keeps glancing at his hands![27]
	Good brother ... Or should I call you Father?[28]

LAY BROTHER	Just brother, – a lay brother, at your service.	535

TEMPLAR	Yes, good brother, if I'd anything
	To give you. But God knows that I have nothing –

LAY BROTHER	Even so, my warmest thanks. God give you	
	Thousandfold what you would like to give.	
	For it is the will and not the gift that makes	540
	The giver. And it wasn't for alms	
	That I was sent to find you, sir.	

TEMPLAR	But you
	Were sent to find me?

LAY BROTHER	Yes, sir, from the monastery.

---

[27] The Templar thinks that this suggests that the Lay Brother wants to ask for alms.

[28] Monks were addressed as *pater* (Father).

TEMPLAR	Where I was hoping now to find a modest
	Pilgrim's meal?
LAY BROTHER	The tables were already 545
	Full; but come back with me now, sir.
TEMPLAR	Why?
	I haven't eaten meat for some time now.
	There's no need anyway. The dates are ripe.
LAY BROTHER	Take care, sir, when you eat this sort of fruit.
	It doesn't do to eat too much, it blocks 550
	The spleen, and makes for melancholy blood.
TEMPLAR	And what if I'm inclined to melancholy?
	But it wasn't just to warn me about this
	That you were sent to me?
LAY BROTHER	Oh no! – I'm
	Just supposed to find out more about you, 555
	Sound you out.
TEMPLAR	You tell me that yourself?
LAY BROTHER	Why not?
TEMPLAR	(A cunning brother, this) – And has
	The monastery more like you?
LAY BROTHER	Don't know.
	I must obey, good sir.
TEMPLAR	And so you just
	Obey and don't ask many questions then? 560
LAY BROTHER	Sir, would I be obedient otherwise?
TEMPLAR	(That shows simplicity is always in
	The right!) Are you allowed to tell me who
	It is who wants to know me better? I would
	Swear it's not yourself.
LAY BROTHER	Would it be fitting 565
	Or of use for me?
TEMPLAR	So who thinks it
	Fitting and of use to be so curious?
LAY BROTHER	The Patriarch, I think. He sent me here
	To look for you.
TEMPLAR	The Patriarch? Surely
	He knows the Templar's white cloak with the red cross 570
	Better than that!
LAY BROTHER	I do!
TEMPLAR	Well then, brother
	I am a Templar and a prisoner –

I'll add that I was captured at the fort
Of Tebnin,[29] which we should have liked to take
Before the ending of the armistice,   575
And then advance on Sidon;[30] furthermore
Of twenty of us captured I alone
Was spared by Saladin; and that is all
The Patriarch should need to know, in fact
More than he needs.

LAY BROTHER   Though hardly more than he   580
Already knows. He'd also like to know
Why Saladin has pardoned you, and you
Alone, sir.

TEMPLAR   Do I know myself? Already
I was kneeling on my cloak, my neck bare,
Waiting for the blow, when Saladin   585
Looked closely at me, stepped near, gave a sign.
Then I was helped up; I was unbound; and I
Wished to thank him. There were tears in
His eyes. He was silent, so was I.
And then he left. I stayed. What all this means   590
The Patriarch can puzzle out.

LAY BROTHER   He thinks
That God has destined you to undertake
The greatest deeds.

TEMPLAR   The greatest deeds! Like
Rescuing a Jewish girl from death by fire!
Acting as a guide on pilgrimage   595
To Sinai;[31] more like that.

LAY BROTHER   There will
Be greater things. So far you've not done badly,
The Patriarch himself already has
Far more important business for you, sir.

TEMPLAR   Really? Do you think so, brother? Has he   600
Told you something?

---

[29]   A fortress near Acre, taken from the Crusaders in 1187.

[30]   Sidon, on the Mediterranean coast belonged to the Crusaders since 1111, but was captured by Saladin in 1187.

[31]   Sinai was said to be the mountain where Moses received the Ten Commandments. Christian pilgrims were allowed to go there.

LAY BROTHER	Yes, he has,

LAY BROTHER   Yes, he has,
I'm told to sound you out, sir, and to see
If you're the man he wants.

TEMPLAR   Well, sound me out!
(I'll see what form this sounding takes) – Well?

LAY BROTHER The quickest way will be to tell you, sir,   605
Exactly what the Patriarch's wishes are.

TEMPLAR   What are they?

LAY BROTHER   He would like you to deliver
A short letter for him, sir.

TEMPLAR   Me? I'm
Not a messenger – Is this the glorious
Deed, more glorious than rescuing   610
A Jewish girl from fire?

LAY BROTHER   It must be. For
The contents of this letter, says the Patriarch,
Are vital to the whole of Christendom.
The safe delivery of this letter – says
The Patriarch – will be rewarded by   615
Our Father with a special crown in Heaven.
No-one – says the Patriarch – is worthier
To wear this crown than you, sir.

TEMPLAR   I?

LAY BROTHER There's hardly anybody – says the Patriarch –
Who's better qualified to earn   620
This crown than you, good sir.

TEMPLAR   Than I?

LAY BROTHER   You're free
Here; you can look around you everywhere;
You understand how to attack or to
Defend a town; you're well placed – says the Patriarch –
To assess the strength and weakness of   625
The inner second wall which Saladin
Has just had built. You could describe it to
The warriors of God in detail, says
The Patriarch.

TEMPLAR   Good brother, could you tell me
More about the contents of this letter?   630

LAY BROTHER Well, I don't know very much about it,
But it is a letter to King Philip.[32]

---

[32] Philippe II (1165–1223), King of France, who had returned to France after the capture of Acre.

The Patriarch ... I've often asked myself
How such a holy man, who dedicates
His life to Heaven, at the same time can   635
Demean himself to be so well informed
Of worldly things. It must be hard for him!

TEMPLAR   Well then? The Patriarch? –

LAY BROTHER   He has precise
And certain knowledge, how and where, and in
What strength, and from which quarter, Saladin   640
Will open his campaign, if war breaks out
Again.

TEMPLAR   He knows that?

LAY BROTHER   Yes, and he would like
To let King Philip know about it too;
To enable him to calculate
How serious a danger there might be,   645
And judge if it is better to renew,
At any cost, the truce with Saladin
Which your courageous Order broke
So recently.

TEMPLAR   Some Patriarch! – I see;
The dear brave man is asking me to be   650
Not just a messenger; he wants a spy! –
Good brother, kindly tell your Patriarch,
As far as you can sound me out, I am
The wrong man for this job. I am obliged
To look upon myself as prisoner.   655
The single duty of the Templar is
To wield his sword with valour on the battlefield,
Not espionage!

LAY BROTHER   Just as I thought! –
And I can't blame you much for that, sir.
Yet the best is still to come. – The Patriarch   660
Has got to know the name, and the location,
Of the fortress in the Lebanon,[33]
Where those enormous sums are stored, which
Saladin's far-sighted father uses
To finance the army and equipment   665
For the war. Now, Saladin from time
To time visits this fortress, travelling
Along deserted roads with little escort –
You're with me?

---

[33]   The German text refers to Mount Lebanon.

TEMPLAR	Never that!	
LAY BROTHER	What could be	

Simpler? All you have to do is capture   670
Saladin, And make an end of him.
You shudder? But already there are two
God-fearing Maronites[34] who have prepared
To risk the deed; they only need a trusty
Man to lead them there.

TEMPLAR   And so the Patriarch   675
Has chosen me to be this trusty man?

LAY BROTHER He thinks likely, from a base in Acre[35]
King Philip would be better able to
Assist our cause.

TEMPLAR   You ask me this? Me?
Did you not hear me, brother, when I told   680
You what a debt of gratitude I owe
To Saladin?

LAY BROTHER   Indeed I heard.

TEMPLAR   And yet?

LAY BROTHER The Patriarch says, That's all very well:
But God and the Order

TEMPLAR   They change nothing! They
Can't order me to villainy!

LAY BROTHER   No.   685
But – says the Patriarch – what's Villainy
To human eyes may not be villainy to God.

TEMPLAR I owe my life to Saladin. And now
I should take his?

LAY BROTHER   But, says the Patriarch,
Saladin is still an enemy   690
Of Christianity who cannot ever
Earn the right to be your friend.

TEMPLAR   My friend?
Because I cannot be a villain to him?
An ungrateful villain?

---

[34] Maronites were members of the Syrian Christian Church, since 1181 associated with the Roman Church.

[35] Acre was conquered by Saladin in 1187, and besieged for three years by the Crusaders.

LAY BROTHER	Why of course! –	
	But – says the Patriarch – we owe no thanks,	695
	In sight of God or humankind, if what	
	Was done to us was not done for our sake.	
	There is a rumour – says the Patriarch –	
	That Saladin has only pardoned you	
	Because he finds a trace of something in	700
	Your looks and bearing not unlike his brother ...	
TEMPLAR	And the Patriarch knows this as well?	
	And what if it were true? Ah Saladin!	
	If nature made *one* feature in me, which	
	Suggested a resemblance to your brother,	705
	Could nothing in my soul then echo it?	
	And how could I suppress that echo just	
	To be obliging to a Patriarch? –	
	Nature, you do not lie! And in His works	
	God does not contradict himself. Go, brother,	710
	Don't provoke my anger! Go! Go!	
LAY BROTHER	I'll go, and I'll go happier than I came.	
	But do forgive me, sir. We in the cloister	
	Are bound to obey the orders of our masters.	

Scene 6

The Templar and Daja, who has been watching the Templar from a distance for a while, and now comes up to him.

DAJA	It seems to me the Brother did not leave	715
	Him in the best of moods. And yet I have	
	To risk my message now.	
TEMPLAR	Oh wonderful!	
	The proverb tells the truth, that monk and woman	
	Are the two claws of the devil! And	
	Today I'm hurled from one claw to the other.	720
DAJA	Is it? Noble knight, it's you? Thank God,	
	A thousand thanks to God. But where have you	
	Been hiding all this time? I trust you've not	
	Been ill?	
TEMPLAR	No.	
DAJA	So you're in good health?	
TEMPLAR	Yes.	
DAJA	We really were quite seriously concerned	725
	About you.	
TEMPLAR	Oh!	
DAJA	You must have gone away?	
TEMPLAR	Correct.	

DAJA	And just returned today?
TEMPLAR	Yesterday.
DAJA	Recha's father came back home today.
	So now may Recha have some hope?
TEMPLAR	Of what?
DAJA	Of the request she often sends to you. 730
	Her father will invite you soon himself
	Most pressingly. He's come from Babylon
	With twenty fully laden camels, bearing
	Every costly thing you could imagine:
	Noble spices, precious stones and cloth, 735
	From India and Persia, Syria
	And even China.
TEMPLAR	I'm not buying anything.
DAJA	He is honoured by his people as
	A prince. And yet I've often wondered why
	They call him 'Wise Nathan' and not 'Nathan 740
	The Rich'.
TEMPLAR	Perhaps to people of his race
	Wise and rich mean just the same.
DAJA	But above
	All, he should be called 'The Good' by them.
	You can't conceive at all how good he is.
	When he found out what Recha owed to you 745
	There was nothing at that moment he would
	Not have done for you, or given you!
TEMPLAR	Oh!
DAJA	Just come and see yourself.
TEMPLAR	See what? How quickly
	Such a moment vanishes?
DAJA	If he
	Were not so good, would I have been prepared 750
	To stay so long with him? Do you think I have
	No feeling for my own worth as a Christian?
	No song at my cradle prophesied
	That I'd accompany my husband here
	To Palestine with no more purpose than 755
	To educate a Jewish girl. You see,
	My husband served as horse soldier
	In Emperor Frederick's[36] army –

---

[36] Emperor Frederick I (1121–90) (Frederick Barbarossa) drowned in the river Saleph in Armenia in 1190.

TEMPLAR	Yes, a Swiss
	By birth, who was vouchsafed the honour and
	The privilege of drowning in a river 760
	With his Imperial Majesty – Yes, woman!
	How often have you told me this before?
	How much longer will you persecute me?

| DAJA | Persecute? Dear God! |

TEMPLAR	Yes, persecute.
	I refuse to see or hear you any 765
	More. I will not be reminded constantly
	Of something which I did without a thought
	And which remains a mystery to me
	When I think about it. Not that I
	Am anxious to regret it. But you see, 770
	Should such a thing occur again, you'd be
	To blame, if I were not so quick to act,
	If I asked questions first, and left to burn
	Whatever was in the flames.

| DAJA | God save us! |

TEMPLAR	From
	Now on, do me the favour of ignoring 775
	Me. That's all I ask. And get the father
	Off my back. A Jew's a Jew. And I'm
	A blunt young Swabian.[37] The image of
	The girl has long since left my mind, if ever
	It was there.

| DAJA | But yours still lives in hers.   780 |

| TEMPLAR | What good can come of it? What good? |

| DAJA | Who knows? |
| | People are not always what they seem. |

| TEMPLAR | But seldom any better. *(He walks away)* |

| DAJA | Wait! Why do |
| | You rush away? |

| TEMPLAR | Woman, don't make me hate |
| | These palm trees, in whose shade I've often walked.   785 |

DAJA	Go away, you German bear, just go –
	But I must not lose track of this wild beast.
	(She follows him at a distance)

---

[37] Swabia is in south-west Germany.

Act II

Scene 1

Saladin and Sittah

(Scene: The Sultan's Palace. Saladin and Sittah are playing chess)

SITTAH Saladin, wake up! What's happened to your game?

SALADIN No good? I thought it was.

SITTAH   Not even for me.
          Take that move back again.

SALADIN   But why?

SITTAH   Your knight   790
          Is unprotected.

SALADIN   Oh True. There then!

SITTAH   Now I can
          Play a fork.[38]

SALADIN   That's true again, so check![39]

SITTAH What good is that? I now move out; and you
          Are as you were.

SALADIN   I see I'm in a trap
          I can't escape without some sacrifice.   795
          Oh well! Just take the knight.

SITTAH   I don't want him
          I shall go past.

SALADIN   That gives me nothing. For
          Your strategy involves more than my knight.

SITTAH Maybe.

SALADIN   Don't start counting chickens before
          They're hatched. There now! How's that? That's not what you 800
          Expected?

SITTAH   No of course. How could I have
          Expected that you'd grown so tired of
          Your queen?

SALADIN   Tired of my queen, you say?

---

[38] A move in which one chess piece threatens two opposing ones.

[39] A threat to take the King.

SITTAH   I see. Today I'll only win my thousand
            Dinars.[40] Not a single Nasarin[41] more.   805

SALADIN   How so?

SITTAH   How can you ask? Because you're trying
            To lose, with all your might. But my account
            Does not gain anything. Besides the fact
            That there's no pleasure in a game like this,
            Have I not always won more from you when   810
            I lost? When I have lost a game, you always
            Have consoled me afterwards by paying
            Double what you really owe me.

SALADIN   I see. So now I've beaten you it's *you* who's
            Lost the game on purpose, little sister?   815

SITTAH   At least, dear little brother, it may be
            That we should blame your generosity
            If I've not learned to play chess any better.

SALADIN   But we neglect our game. Let's finish it.

SITTAH   As you were? Check! And double check!   820

SALADIN   I admit I never noticed this
            Discovered check, which also takes away
            My queen.

SITTAH   Could you have stopped it happening?
            Let's see.

SALADIN   No, no; just take the queen away.
            I wasn't really happy with this piece.   825

SITTAH   Just with that piece?

SALADIN   Away with it! It doesn't
            Matter. Every piece is covered once
            Again.

SITTAH   My brother has instructed me
            Too well how courteously one must behave
            To queens.[42] (*She leaves the piece*)

SALADIN   Then take it or don't take it! It's   830
            The only one I have.

---

[40]   A Dinar was an Arabian gold coin.

[41]   A Nasarin was a small silver coin.

[42]   Saladin had allowed Queen Sybille to visit her captured husband, Guy de
Lusignan, King of Jerusalem.

SITTAH	No need to take it.
	Check! Check!
SALADIN	Go on then.
SITTAH	Check! and check! and check!
SALADIN	Checkmate!
SITTAH	Not quite; your knight can move between

Them; or whatever else you like. It won't
Make any difference.

SALADIN	Quite right, You've won: 835

Al-Hafi pays. Let him be called! At once!
Sittah, you weren't far wrong; I wasn't concentrating
On the game: I was preoccupied.
And who keeps giving us this set of faceless
Pieces?[43] One can't memorize them, they are   840
Characterless. Have I been playing against
The Imam?[44] But a loss must seek excuses.
I admit the shapeless pieces didn't
Make me lose; it was your skill, the greater
Calm and sharpness of your judgement ...

SITTAH	Now 845

You want to blunt the sting of your defeat.
It's just that you were more preoccupied
Than even I was.

SALADIN	What preoccupied *your* mind?
SITTAH	Not your preoccupation! Saladin,

When shall we have a serious game again?   850

SALADIN	We'll play it yet more keenly when we do!

You mean because the war restarts? Let it!
I was not the first to take up arms;
I wish we could extend the truce again.
And at the same time I'd have liked so much   855
To give my Sittah a good husband
This must be Richard's[45] brother;[46] after all
He is *Richard's* brother.

---

[43] The Koran forbids the use of images, so that strict Muslims would play with marked stones.

[44] The Imam, as the leader in a mosque, would be strict on this point.

[45] Richard I (1157–99) (Coeur de Lion).

[46] Prince John, later King John (1166–1216).

SITTAH   How you love to praise
             Your Richard!

SALADIN   And if Richard's sister
             Had become our brother Melek's[47] wife,   860
             Then what a dynasty that would have made!
             The first and best of all the world's great dynasties
             You hear, I'm quite prepared to praise myself
             As well; I think I'm worthy of my friends,
             What men and women would have sprung from that!   865

SITTAH   Have I not also smiled at this fair dream?
             You cannot, will not, understand the Christians.
             Their pride is: to be Christian, but not human.
             Even that mixture of humanity
             And superstition, which their founder gave to them,   870
             They love not for it's human values,
             But because Christ teaches it, Christ did it.
             It's well for them he was so good a human
             Being. And it's well for them that they
             Can take his virtue in good faith. And yet   875
             What virtue? Not his virtue; it's his name
             That must be spread throughout the world, that must
             Dishonour and devour the names of all
             Good people. For the name, the name alone,
             Is everything to them.

SALADIN   You mean to say,   880
             Why else would they demand of you and Melek
             That each of you should bear the name of Christians[48]
             If you want to love a Christian as a spouse?

SITTAH   Yes. As if that love, which our Creator
             Granted every man and woman, could   885
             Be expected only of a Christian?

SALADIN   Christians believe in such absurdities
             That they could easily believe in that.
             But all the same, you're wrong. The Templars, not
             The Christians are to blame; They are to blame   890
             As Templars, not as Christians, Just because
             Of them, the whole plan fails. They want Acre,
             Which Richard's sister was to bring as dowry
             To our brother Melek, and they *will* not

---

[47]   In 1192 Richard I agreed on a three-year armistice with Saladin. The marriage
plan was to consolidate this.

[48]   A condition was that Melek should convert to Christianity.

Let it go. In order not to lose 895
The advantage of the knight, they play the monk,
The foolish monk. And they could hardly wait
Until the ending of the armistice
To try their luck with a surprise attack.
How splendid! Carry on dear gentlemen, 900
Just carry on! It's all the same to me.
If only other things went as they ought.

SITTAH   Oh?
What else has disconcerted you? What else
Has put you out of humour so?

SALADIN   The same
That always put me out of humour in 905
The past. I was in Lebanon with father.
He is overwhelmed with problems.

SITTAH   Oh dear!

SALADIN He cannot cope; he's hemmed in everywhere,
He lacks so much.

SITTAH   Hemmed in? What does he lack?

SALADIN What I cannot bring myself to name, 910
Which, when I have it, seems superfluous,
And if I don't, seems indispensable.
Where is Al-Hafi then? Has no one gone
To find him? Wretched and accursed money!
Hafi! Good! I'm glad you're here.

Scene 2

The dervish Al-Hafi, Saladin and Sittah

AL-HAFI   The money 915
Has arrived from Egypt, I suppose.
I hope there's plenty of it.

SALADIN   Have you news?

AL-HAFI   I?
I haven't. I was thinking I'd receive
Some news from you.

SALADIN   Pay Sittah a thousand
Dinars. *(Walking up and down thinking)*

AL-HAFI   Pay instead of being paid! 920
Just fine! that's something even less than nothing.
To Sittah? once again to Sittah? And
You've lost? You have lost at chess again? Is this
The game here still?

SITTAH	At least you must admit
	My luck.

AL-HAFI *(looking at the game)*
                     Admit what? But surely you know ...   925

SITTAH *(signals to him)*
            Sh! Hafi! Sh!

AL-HAFI *(still looking at the game)*
                     You're too quick off the mark!

SITTAH Al-Hafi! Sh!

AL-HAFI *(to Sittah)*
                     So you were playing white?
            And you called check?

SITTAH   He hasn't heard, thank God.

AL-HAFI Now it's his move?

SITTAH *(going up to him)*
                     Just say to Saladin
            That I can have my money.

AL-HAFI *(still absorbed by the game)*
                                         Yes, of course   930
            You shall receive it, as you always do.

SITTAH What, are you mad?

AL-HAFI   The game's not over yet.
            You really haven't lost it, Saladin.

SALADIN *(hardly listening)*
            Just pay! Just Pay!

AL-HAFI   Pay! Pay!
            Your queen is still in place.

SALADIN *(as before)*
                                         It makes no odds;   935
            It isn't in the game now.

SITTAH   Oh come on!
            Just say that I can have the money now.

AL-HAFI *(still absorbed by the game)*
            That's understood, as usual – All the same,
            Even if the queen is not in play, it's
            Not yet checkmate.

SALADIN *(steps forward and overthrows the board)*
                                         Yes it is. That's how   940
            I want it.

AL-HAFI   Yes, your game is like her winnings!
            Paid as it was won.

SALADIN   *(to Sittah)*
                    What's that he says?

SITTAH   *(making signs to Al-Hafi from time to time)*
   You know him, how he bristles, likes to be
   Consulted, a bit envious perhaps.

SALADIN   Surely not of you? Not of my sister?   945
   What's this, Al-Hafi? Envious? You?

AL-HAFI   Perhaps,
   Perhaps! I think I'd rather have her brain;
   I'd rather be as good as her.

SITTAH   But even
   So, he's always paid the right amount,
   And he will pay today as well. Just leave him!   950
   Go, Al-Hafi, go. I'll send out for
   The money later.

AL-HAFI   No. I won't keep up
   This farce with you. He must be told the truth
   Sometime.

SALADIN   Who? Told what truth?

SITTAH   Al-Hafi!
   Is this your promise? Do you keep your word   955
   To me like this?

AL-HAFI   How could I know, that it
   Would go so far.

SALADIN   And am I to be told
   Nothing?

SITTAH   Al-Hafi, do please be discreet.

SALADIN   But this is very strange. Just what could Sittah
   Want to beg so solemnly and fervently   960
   From a foreigner, and from a dervish,
   Rather than from me, from her own brother.
   Al-Hafi, I command you now. Speak, dervish.

SITTAH   Brother, don't let a trifle of this kind
   Concern you more than it deserves.   965
   You know, that several times I've won the same
   Amount from you when we played chess. Well then,
   Because I have no urgent need of it,
   And as the funds in Hafi's coffers aren't
   Exactly overflowing, just because   970
   Of this, the sums have not been paid. Don't worry,
   I'm not intending to donate them to you,
   Brother, nor to Hafi, nor the coffers.

AL-HAFI   Yes, but that's not all!

SITTAH	And other sums

SITTAH   And other sums
Like that; they too are still unpaid. And also   975
Your allowance to me has remained
Untouched for several months.

AL-HAFI   That's still
Not all.

SALADIN   Not all? Speak out! Just tell me then!

AL-HAFI While we've been waiting for the gold from Egypt,
She has ...

SITTAH *(to Saladin)*
                   Why listen to him?

AL-HAFI   She's not only   980
Taken nothing ...

SALADIN   Good girl! She has helped out
With advances, hasn't she?

AL-HAFI   Maintained
The whole court; covered your expenses single-
Handed.

SALADIN   Ah, how like my own dear sister!
(embraces her)

SITTAH And who has made me rich enough to do   985
This, but my brother?

AL-HAFI   Soon he'll make a pauper
Of her once again, just like he is
Himself.

SALADIN   I, poor? Your brother, poor? But when
Have I had more? And when have I had less?
One coat, one sword, one horse, one God! What more 990
Do I need if I have as much as this?
And yet, Al-Hafi, I've a mind to scold you.

SITTAH Brother, don't scold. I only wish I could
Relieve our father in his troubles too.

SALADIN Ah! Now at once you have destroyed my cheerful 995
Mood again. Though I need nothing for
Myself, and can need nothing, he is in
Great need and through him we are too. So what
Am I to do? Perhaps nothing will come
From Egypt for a long time. Why that is,   1000
God knows. For all is peaceful there. I can
Reduce, retrench, economise, and do it
With a will, if it affects no-one
But me, just me alone, and no one else
Is made to suffer. And yet what can that   1005

Achieve? One horse, one coat, one sword, I still
Must have. And I can't gain by bargaining
With God. For he asks very little of
Me – just my heart. All I was counting on
Was any surplus from your treasury,   1010
Al-Hafi.

AL-HAFI   Surplus? Tell me, would you not
Have had me run-through, or at least have had
Me strangled, if you had discovered that
I had been holding back a surplus. No
I'd rather risk embezzlement than that.   1015

SALADIN   But what are we to do then? Could you not
Have borrowed first from someone else instead
of Sittah?

SITTAH   Do you think I'd let him take
This privilege away from me, my brother?
And I still insist on it. I'm not   1020
Quite bankrupt yet.

SALADIN   Not quite? That's the last straw!
Go off at once, Al-Hafi, make a start.
Take from anyone you can; and how you can.
Go, borrow, promise. But don't borrow from
The people I made rich. For borrowing   1025
From them might seem like taking back a gift.
Go to the greatest misers; they're the ones
Who'll gladly lend to me. They understand
How well their money prospers in my hands.

AL-HAFI   I know no one like that.

SITTAH   It just occurs   1030
To me that I have heard, Al-Hafi, that
Your friend has come back.

AL-HAFI   *(disconcerted)*
                            Friend? My friend? And who
Might that be?

SITTAH   The Jew you highly praised.

AL-HAFI   A Jew I praised? And highly?

SITTAH   To whom God –
I still remember clearly the expression   1035
Which you used about him once – to whom
His God has granted both the smallest and
The greatest of the treasures of this world
In full measure.

AL-HAFI	Did I say that? What did
	I mean by that?

SITTAH   The smallest riches. And   1040
The greatest wisdom.

AL-HAFI   What? About a Jew?
Could I have said all that about a Jew?

SITTAH You said of your Nathan, didn't you?

AL-HAFI Oh yes! Of him! Of Nathan! He just didn't
Spring to mind. So is it really true?   1045
He's come back home again at last? Well! He
Cannot be badly off in that case. You're
Quite right: the people once called him 'the Wise',
'The Rich' as well.

SITTAH   'The Rich' now, even more
Than ever. All the town resounds with talk   1050
Of all the precious things, the treasures he
Has brought back.

AL-HAFI   Well, if he's 'the Rich' again,
He's probably 'the Wise' again as well.

SITTAH Al-Hafi, do you think you could approach him?

AL-HAFI But for what? You can't mean for a loan?   1055
You don't know him. He won't lend. His wisdom
Is that he will never lend to anyone.

SITTAH But you gave me quite a different view
Of him before.

AL-HAFI   If necessary, he
Will lend you goods. But money? Never, No   1060
He's quite unlike the usual kind of Jew.
He possesses understanding, he's
Well mannered, plays good chess. But he stands out
Among all other Jews in bad ways just
As much as good. You really cannot count   1065
On him. He certainly gives money to
The poor, perhaps as much as Saladin,
Or if not quite as much, as willingly.
Without discrimination too; Jew, Christian,
Muslim, Parsee,[49] they are all alike   1070
To him.

---

[49]   Parsee – Indian follower of Zoroaster, founder of the Persian cult of fire.

SITTAH	And such a man ...
SALADIN	How can it be That I have never heard about this man?
SITTAH	Would he refuse to lend to Saladin, Who needs it on behalf of others, not Himself?

AL-HAFI   But here you see the Jew again,   1075
The common Jew. Believe me, he is jealous
Of your generosity. He envies
You! In all the world, when ever someone
Says 'God reward you', he would like it to
Be said to him. That's why he doesn't lend,   1080
So that he always has enough to give.
Because his law^{50} commands him to be charitable,
But does not order him to be obliging.
Charity makes him the least obliging
Fellow in the world. For quite a while now   1085
My relations with him have been somewhat
Strained. But just because of that, you mustn't
Ever think that I don't do him justice.
He is good for everything, except for this;
For this he really is no good. I'll go   1090
And knock on other doors at once. I know
A Moor, I've just remembered, who is rich
And miserly, I'll go. I'll go and see him.

SITTAH	What's the hurry, -Hafi?
SALADIN	Let him go!

Scene 3
Sittah and Saladin

SITTAH   He's rushing off as if he's glad to get   1095
Away from me. Why? Has he been deceived
By Nathan, or are we the ones he wishes to
Deceive?

SALADIN   Why do you ask me? I hardly know
Who you were talking of. Until today
I never heard a thing about this Jew   1100
Of yours, this Nathan.

SITTAH   Can it be that such
A man is still unknown to you? They say
He has explored the tombs of Solomon

---

^{50} The Mosaic law.

And David,[51] and he knows a mighty magic
Word with which he can remove their seals.   1105
From them he brings out to the light of day
From time to time those untold riches which
Could not have come from any other source.

SALADIN   If this man took his riches out of tombs
They certainly were not from Solomon's   1110
or David's tombs. Fools must be buried there!

SITTAH   Or scoundrels! And in any case
His source of riches is more fruitful, and
More inexhaustible, than a mere tomb,
Full of Mammon.[52]

SALADIN   He's a merchant then.   1115

SITTAH   His camels travel on all roads, and go
Across all deserts. Nathan's ships are to
Be found in every harbour. I was told that
By Al-Hafi. And he added with
Delight how great and noble was the use   1120
His friend made of the wealth which he acquired
With skill and energy. How nothing was
Too small, how free his mind was from all prejudice,
How open was his heart to every virtue,
And how he was attuned to every beauty.   1125

SALADIN   But Al-Hafi spoke of him so coldly, so
Uncertainly.

SITTAH   Not coldly, more embarrassed,
As if he thought it dangerous to praise him,
But did not want to be unjustly critical.
Or could it be that, even though he is   1130
The best of all his people he cannot
Help being one of them? Perhaps Al-Hafi
Feels ashamed of him in this respect.
Well, be that as it may. It doesn't matter
If the Jew is more or less like other   1135
Jews. He's rich, and that's enough for us.

SALADIN   But surely, sister, you do not intend
To take what's his by force?

SITTAH   What do you mean
By force? With fire and sword? Of course not. With

---

[51]   A reference to a legend that treasures were buried in these graves.

[52]   Mammon-riches.

The weak the only kind of force one needs 1140
Is their own weakness. Now just come with me
To hear a singer in my harem whom
I purchased only yesterday. Perhaps
Meanwhile I can work out a strategy
I have for dealing with this Nathan. Come! 1145

Scene 4

Recha, Nathan and Daja
    (Scene: In front of Nathan's house, where it meets the palm trees. Recha and Nathan come out. Daja joins them.)

RECHA   Father, you have been so long. There's little 1146
    Chance of meeting him by now.

NATHAN   Well, well;
    If we've missed him here, beneath the palms,
    We'll see him somewhere else. Be calm now. Look!
    Is that not Daja coming to us?

RECHA   She 1150
    Will surely have lost sight of him by now.

NATHAN   I doubt it.

RECHA   Then she would be walking faster.

NATHAN   Probably she hasn't seen us.

RECHA   Now
    She's seen us.

NATHAN   Look, she's coming twice as fast.
    So just calm down.

RECHA   You wouldn't really want 1155
    A daughter who was calm at such a moment?
    Who did not want to know to whose good deed
    She owes her life? Her life which she loves only
    Because she owes it first of all to you.

NATHAN   I wouldn't want you different from what 1160
    You are; not even if I understand
    That something new is stirring in your soul.

RECHA   What, father?

NATHAN   You ask me so shyly? That
    Which now develops in your inmost heart
    Is innocence and nature. Let it cause you 1165
    No distress. It causes none to me.
    But promise one thing to me; if your heart
    Declares itself more openly, don't hide
    Its wishes from me.

RECHA	I tremble at the very Thought that I might hide my heart from you.	1170
NATHAN	No more about this, it is settled now And for all time. But here is Daja. Well?	
DAJA	He's still here, walking in the palm-grove. Soon He'll come out from behind that wall. Look, Here he comes!	
RECHA	Ah! He looks undecided. Where now? Further on? Or back? Or to the right? Or left?	1175
DAJA	No, no. He's sure to take a few more turns Around the monastery. And after that, I'm sure he'll pass us here.	
RECHA	That's right! But did You speak to him? How did he seem?	
DAJA	As always.	1180
NATHAN	Make sure he doesn't know that you are here. Go further back. Or better still go right Inside.	
RECHA	Just one more look! Oh, no, the hedge Is hiding him from me.	
DAJA	Come on. Your father Is quite right. If he should see you, he Might turn back straight away.	1185
RECHA	That hedge again!	
NATHAN	And if he comes out from behind it suddenly, He is bound to see you. He can't help it. So Hurry, go!	
DAJA	Come on; I know a window Where we can see what they are doing.	
RECHA	Yes?	1190
	(Both go inside)	

Scene 5

Nathan soon joined by the Templar

NATHAN	I'm almost frightened of this strange young man. His rugged virtue almost makes me hesitate. But how can one man make another feel So ill at ease? Ah! Here he comes. By God, He's certainly a manly youth. I like	1195

His good, defiant look, and his firm step.
However bitter is his shell, the kernel
Cannot be. Where have I seen his like?
Forgive me, noble Frank.

TEMPLAR   What?

NATHAN   Please allow me.

TEMPLAR   What, Jew, what?

NATHAN   To venture to address you.   1200

TEMPLAR   How can I prevent it? But you'd better
Make it short.

NATHAN   Please wait. Don't rush away
So proudly and contemptuously from
A man who is forever in your debt.

TEMPLAR   How's that? Ah, I believe I know. You are ...   1205

NATHAN   My name is Nathan. I'm the father of
The girl you generously rescued from
The fire. I've come ...

TEMPLAR   To thank me? But I have
Already had to suffer too much thanks
For this mere trifle. As for you, you owe   1210
Me nothing. After all I did not know
That this girl was your daughter. And it is
The duty of the Templar Knights to spring
To the assisstance of all people in
Distress. In any case my life was at   1215
That moment burdensome to me. So I
Was very glad to seize the opportunity
To put my life at risk to save another.
Even if the life I saved might be
As unimportant as this Jewish girl's.   1220

NATHAN   A great and dreadful thing! I think
I understand. Your modest greatness hides
Behind such dreadful words in order
To escape from admiration. All the same
If admiration meets with your contempt   1225
What can we offer that you would find less
Despicable? Sir, if you weren't a stranger
Here, a prisoner, I would not be
So bold in asking you. Give your command:
How can we serve you?

TEMPLAR   You? with nothing.

NATHAN   I'm   1230
              A man with riches.

TEMPLAR   But a richer Jew
              Is not a better Jew to me.

NATHAN   But even so
              Could you not make use of all the good
              Things which he has? Could you not use his riches?

TEMPLAR   Well, I won't reject that out of hand,   1235
              If only for the sake of my old cloak.
              As soon as it wears out, and neither seam
              Nor tatter holds together any longer,
              Then I'll borrow cloth or money from you
              For a new one. But don't look so black!   1240
              You're still quite safe. It isn't that far gone.
              You can see it's still in quite good
              Condition. Only this one corner has
              An ugly mark: that's where it has been singed.
              That happened when I carried out your daughter   1245
              Through the fire.

NATHAN   *(takes hold of the corner of the cloth and looks at it)*
                                How strange it is that such
              An evil stain, the mark of fire, should give
              A man a better testimonial
              Than his own mouth. And I would like to kiss
              This mark. Ah! Pardon me! I couldn't help it.

TEMPLAR   What?

NATHAN   A tear fell on it.

TEMPLAR   Never mind.
              There have been many drops before. (This Jew
              Is disconcerting.)

NATHAN   I wonder if you would
              Be very kind and let your cloak be taken
              Some time to my daughter?

TEMPLAR   For what reason?   1255

NATHAN   So she may press her lips upon this mark.
              For I suppose her wish to fall upon
              Her knees in front of you is now in vain.

TEMPLAR   But Jew, – your name is Nathan? Nathan then,
              You frame your words with skill, and very pointedly   1260
              I am embarrassed – anyway – I would …

NATHAN   React and play a part, just as you wish.

I'll still see through it. You were far too good
And honest to be more polite. The girl
Was all emotion; while the woman messenger   1265
Was too insistent, and the father, far
Away. You were concerned for her good name.
You fled, to save her from an ordeal or defeat.
I thank you for that too.

TEMPLAR   I see you know
The way in which we Templars ought to think.   1270

NATHAN   Why only Templars? And why *ought* to think?
Because it is commanded by the Order?
I know how all good people think, and that
Good people are produced in every land.

TEMPLAR   And yet, I hope, with differences.

NATHAN   Of course   1275
They're different in colour, dress, and build.

TEMPLAR   In one place more, and in another less.

NATHAN   These differences don't amount to much.
Everywhere a great man needs much space,
When several are planted close together   1280
They just break each others' branches. Average
Men like us are countless everywhere.
And yet each one must tolerate the rest,
And yet one gnarled branch must accept another.
And yet no single treetop must presume   1285
That it alone did not spring from the ground.

TEMPLAR   Well spoken! But you also know the race
Which first evolved this petty, carping view
Of humankind? You know which people was
The first to call itself the chosen people,[53] Nathan?   1290
I don't exactly hate this people, but
I cannot help despising them for all
Their pride. Their pride, which they passed down to
Christian and to Muslim, that their God alone
Is the true God!. You are amazed that I,   1295
A Christian and a Templar, speak like this?
When and where has pious fury claimed
More stridently to have the better God,
And to impose it on the whole world as

---

[53] Deuteronomy 7:6. 'The Lord thy God hath chosen thee to be a special people unto himself above all people that are upon the face of the earth.'

The best? Where has it shown itself in blacker   1300
Form than here, and now? Can anybody,
Here and now, be so blinkered ... Leave
Them to their blindness! Just forget what I
Have said, and let me be. *(He is about to go)*

NATHAN   Ah, you don't know
How much more firmly I shall press myself   1305
Upon you now. We really must be friends.
Despise my people if you wish. But neither
Of us chose our people. Are we then
Our people? What does 'people' mean?
Are Jew and Christian, Jew and Christian first   1310
And human beings second? Have I found
In you a man who needs no other name
Than human being?

TEMPLAR   Yes, by God, You're right!
Nathan give me your hand. I am ashamed
That I misjudged you even for a moment.   1315

NATHAN   I'm proud of it. For only common things
Are recognised at once.

TEMPLAR   But what is rare
Is harder to forget. Nathan, of course
We must, we must be friends.

NATHAN   We are already.
How my Recha will rejoice at this!   1320
And what a joyful prospect opens up
Before my eyes! Just get to know her first.

TEMPLAR   I already long to do so. Who is that
Who rushes from your house. Is it not Daja?

NATHAN   Yes, and she looks anxious.

TEMPLAR   Let us hope   1325
Our Recha is all right.

Scene 6

Nathan, Templar and Daja

DAJA   Nathan, Nathan!

NATHAN   Well?

DAJA   Forgive me, noble knight, for interrupting
You.

NATHAN   What is it?

TEMPLAR	Yes, what is it?	
DAJA	The Sultan sends for you. The Sultan wants To speak to you. My God, the Sultan!	
NATHAN	Me? The Sultan? I expect he wants to see What new things I've brought back. Just tell him that Little – almost nothing – is unpacked.	1330
DAJA	No, no, he won't see anything. He wants To speak to you in person, and as soon As possible.	1335
NATHAN	I'll come. Go in, go in!	
DAJA	Please do not be offended, noble knight – God, we are so worried about what The Sultan wants.	
NATHAN	We'll soon find out. Just go!	

Scene 7

Nathan and the Templar

TEMPLAR	So you don't know him yet? I mean in person?	1340
NATHAN	Saladin? Not yet. I've not avoided Meeting him, but never sought him out. The general report spoke so much good Of him that I preferred believing it To meeting him himself. But if it's true That he, by granting you your life …	1345
TEMPLAR	Quite right. At least that's true. The life which I'm now living Is his gift.	
NATHAN	And with this gift he's given Me a double, threefold life. It changes Everything between us. All at once It threw a rope around me, so that I Am bound forever to his service, now. I can scarcely, scarcely wait to hear What he will first command me. I am ready To do anything. And I am ready To admit I do it for your sake.	1350 1355
TEMPLAR	I've had no chance to thank him for myself yet, Even though I've often crossed his path. The impression which I made on him Came suddenly, and disappeared as fast.	1360

Who knows if he remembers me at all.
And yet he must remember me again.
Once more at least; for he must finally
Decide my fate. It's not enough that I
Still live at his command, and at his will.   1365
I now must learn from him according to
Whose will I have to live my life henceforth.

NATHAN   Exactly; one more reason why I won't
Delay. Perhaps a word may give me a chance
To mention you. Forgive me, I must hurry.   1370
But when shall we see you at our house?

TEMPLAR   As soon as you allow.

NATHAN   Or you would like.

TEMPLAR   Today then.

NATHAN   And your name, if I may ask.

TEMPLAR   My name was – is – Curd von Stauffen. Curd.

NATHAN   Von Stauffen? – Stauffen? – Stauffen?

TEMPLAR   Why are you   1375
So struck by that?

NATHAN   Von Stauffen? – There must be
Some other families of that name …

TEMPLAR   Oh yes, there were
More of them – and some rot here to this day.
My uncle himself – my father, I should say –
Why are you looking at me more and more   1380
Intently?

NATHAN   Nothing, nothing. It's just that
I cannot tire of seeing you.

TEMPLAR   Then I
Shall leave you first. The eyes of one who seeks
Have often found more than he wished to find.
I fear them, Nathan. Let time, and not curiosity,   1385
Develop our acquaintance step by step. *(He goes out)*

NATHAN   *(Looking after him in astonishment)*
'The eyes of one who seeks have often found
More than he wished to find'. It is as if
He read my mind. It really is. And yet
It could be possible. He has not only   1390
Wolf's build, Wolf's walk – his voice too is the same
Wolf even used to toss his head like that.

Wolf held his sword as he does, and like him
He also stroked his eyebrows with his hand,
As if to hide the fire in his eyes.   1395
How such images, so deeply etched,
Can sometimes sleep in us, until a single
Word, a sound, awakens them. Von Stauffen –
Right, that's right! Von Filnek and Von Stauffen.
Soon I'll find out more about that, soon,   1400
But first to Saladin. What's this? Is that
Not Daja lurking there? Come closer, Daja.

Scene 8

Daja and Nathan

NATHAN   I suppose that both of you are bursting to
           Discover something very different from
           Why the Sultan wants to see me.

DAJA   Can   1405
           You blame her? You had just begun to talk
           To him more confidentially, when we
           Were driven from the window by the Sultan's
           Messenger.

NATHAN   Just tell her then, she may
           Expect him any moment.

DAJA   Really? Really?   1410

NATHAN   I hope I can rely upon you Daja?
           Please be on your guard. You won't have any
           Reason to regret it, and your conscience
           Will be satisfied by this. But please
           Do nothing to disrupt my plan. Just talk   1415
           And ask your questions with discretion and
           Restraint …

DAJA   I hardly need reminding of
           That. I'm going; you must go yourself.
           But look! I do believe a second messenger
           Has come from Saladin, your dervish, Al-Hafi. *(Exit)* 1420

Scene 9

Nathan and Al-Hafi

AL-HAFI   There you are! It's you I've come to see.

NATHAN   Why this urgency? What does he want
           Of me?

AL-HAFI	Who?

NATHAN   Saladin. I'm on my way.

AL-HAFI   To whom? To Saladin?

NATHAN   Did Saladin
             Not send you?

AL-HAFI   No. Me? Has he sent for you   1425
             Already?

NATHAN   Yes, he has.

AL-HAFI   You mean it's true.

NATHAN   What? What is true?

AL-HAFI   That ... I am not to blame.
             God knows I'm not to blame. The things I've said,
             The lies I've told about you to prevent it!

NATHAN   To prevent what? What is true?

AL-HAFI   That you   1430
             Have now become his treasurer. I pity
             You. But I won't stay to watch. I'm off.
             I leave within the hour. You know where to
             Already, and you know the road. So if
             You have some errands for me on the way,   1435
             Just say; I'm at your service. But I can't
             Take more goods than a naked man can carry.
             I'm going, so be quick.

NATHAN   Al-Hafi, wait.
             Remember I know nothing of all of this.
             What are you going on about?

AL-HAFI   You'll take   1440
             The bag along with you?

NATHAN   The bag?

AL-HAFI   The gold.
             You are supposed to lend to Saladin.

NATHAN   And is that all?

AL-HAFI   Do you expect me to
             Stand by and simply watch how, day by day,
             He bleeds you white? Do you expect me to   1445
             Stand by while his extravagance just borrows,
             Borrows, borrows from the stores of your
             Wise charity, which never failed before,
             Until the poor mice born in them are starving?

Perhaps you might imagine that a man 1450
Who needs your money would consider taking
Your advice? You really think so? Saladin
Accept advice! When has he taken any
Advice? You can't imagine, Nathan, what
Occurred just now when I was with him.

NATHAN   Well? 1455

AL-HAFI   I came to him just after he had played
Chess with his sister. Sittah doesn't play
So badly. And the game, which Saladin
Believed he'd lost, and had conceded, was
Still set out, untouched. I take a look, 1460
And see the game is very far from lost.

NATHAN   That must have been a lucky find for you!

AL-HAFI   All that he had to do was to move the king
Behind the pawn, and out of check. If I
Could only show you!

NATHAN   I believe you. 1465

AL-HAFI   Then the rook was free to move – and she
Was lost. I wanted to explain it to him.
I called him. Guess what?

NATHAN   And he disagreed?

AL-HAFI   He wouldn't even listen, but with scorn
He turned the whole game over.

NATHAN   How could he? 1470

AL-HAFI   He said he *wanted* to be checkmate anyway.
He wanted to! You call that playing chess?

NATHAN   No, playing *with* the game.

AL-HAFI   And it was worth
A pretty penny.

NATHAN   Money, money, money!
That's the least of it. But to refuse 1475
To listen to Al-Hafi, and to shut
His ears to you on such a weighty point,
Not to appreciate your eagle eye:
That cries aloud for vengence, does it not?

AL-HAFI   Now, now, I'm only telling you all this 1480
So you can see what sort of head he has.
In short, I cannot stand him any longer.
So I've been chasing all the Moorish sharks
And asking who will make a loan to him.

I, who've never begged a penny for   1485
Myself, must borrow for another. Borrowing
Is much the same as begging, just as lending
For the interest is much the same
As stealing. With my Ghebers[54] on the Ganges
I don't need either, and I need not be   1490
The tool of either. On the Ganges, on
The Ganges, only there are human beings.
You alone, of all those here, are worthy
To live beside the Ganges. Will you come
With me? Leave all your trash to him and let   1495
Him deal with it. He'll get it from you
Anyway by degrees. This way you'll lose
Your burden all at once. I'll get a delk[55]
For you. Come on!

NATHAN   I think we'll always have
This choice, Al-Hafi, but I want to think   1500
It over. Wait …

AL-HAFI   What? Think about it?
No thought is needed for a thing like this.

NATHAN   But only till I get back from the Sultan;
Until I've said goodbye …

AL-HAFI   Whoever thinks
About it seeks excuses not to act.   1505
If he can't instantly decide to live
Just for himself, he'll always be a slave
To others. As you wish. Farewell. Just as
You like. I'll go my way, you go yours.

NATHAN   Al-Hafi! You will put your own affairs   1510
In order first?

AL-HAFI   Oh nonsense! Any cash
That's left is hardly worth the counting. My
Accounts are guaranteed by you or Sittah.
Farewell! *(Exit)*

NATHAN   *(looking after him)*
                  I'll guarantee them. Wild, good, noble –
How can I describe him? In the end,   1515
A real beggar is the only real king!
(Exit the other side.)

---

[54]   Ghebers – Persian name for followers of Zoroaster, also called Parsees (see Act II, Sc.2).

[55]   delk – the Arabian name for the dervish dress.

Act III

Scene 1
Recha and Daja
Scene: (in Nathan's house)

RECHA	What was it, Daja, that my father said
	To us? "You can expect him any moment".
	Don't you think that sounds as if he will
	Arrive here very soon? How many moments 1520
	Have already passed! – But then, why think
	Of vanished moments? All I want now is
	To live each passing moment as it comes.
	At last will come the one which brings him here.
DAJA	Curse that message from the Sultan! If 1525
	It weren't for that I'm sure that Nathan would
	Have brought him right away.
RECHA	And when this moment
	Comes at last, and when it brings with it
	Fulfilment of the warmest and the deepest
	Of my wishes – what then? What then?
DAJA	What then? 1530
	Then I hope the warmest of *my* wishes
	Will achieve fulfilment too.
RECHA	But then what will
	Replace this wish within my heart? It has
	Forgotten how to feel unless it has
	One overpowering wish. Will there be – nothing? 1535
	Oh, it frightens me!
DAJA	Then my own wish
	Will take the place of yours, once yours is satisfied –
	My wish to know that you will be in Europe
	In the care of people worthy of you.
RECHA	How wrong you are! The very reason which 1540
	Creates this wish in you prevents it ever
	Being mine. You feel the pull of your
	Own homeland. Should not *my* land hold me here?
	Why should a vision of your people, which
	Has not yet faded from your mind, have greater 1545
	Influence than people I can see,
	Touch, hear – *my* people?
DAJA	Pointless to resist.
	The ways of Heaven are the ways of Heaven.
	And suppose your Templar were to be

The means by which his God, for whom he fights,   1550
Intends to lead you to the land and to
The people for whom you were born?

RECHA   O Daja!
What are you saying yet again, dear Daja!
You really do have most peculiar
Ideas! 'His God, *his* God for whom he fights.'   1555
To whom does God belong? What sort of God
Belongs to just one person? One who needs
People to fight for him? And how can we
Know which bit of earth we have been born for,
Unless it is the one *on* which we have   1560
Been born? If father were to hear you talk!
What has he done to you that you must always
See my happiness so far from him?
What has he done to make you want to mix
The seed of pure reason,[56] which he planted   1565
In my soul, with weeds or flowers of
Your homeland? Dear, beloved Daja, he
Does not want your brightly coloured flowers
In my soil now; and I have to tell you
That however beautifully they   1570
May cover it, I feel my soil has been
So weakened, so impoverished by all
Your flowers; in their scent, their sweet-sour scent
I feel so dizzy and so numb. – Your brain
Is more accustomed to this. I don't blame you   1575
For your stronger nerves, which can endure it.
But it's not for me. As for your "Angel" –
Did it not so very nearly make a fool
Of me? This nonsense makes me feel ashamed
In front of my own father.

DAJA   Nonsense? – as if   1580
This place were blessed with reason! Nonsense!
If only I could speak!

RECHA   Are you not free
To speak? Did I not always listen when
You chose to talk to me about the heroes
Of your own religion? Have I ever   1585
Failed to admire their deeds, to shed tears gladly
For their sufferings? It's true, I did not

---

[56] Matthew 13:24. 'The Kingdom of Heaven is likened unto a man which sowed good seed in his field.'

Think their faith the most heroic quality
In them. What I found more consoling was
The lesson that devotedness to God   1590
Does not wholly depend on what
We speculate about him. Dear Daja,
My father has so often told us that;
And you have often said that you agreed
With him. So why do you now undermine   1595
Alone what you have built with him
Together? – Dear Daja, this is not the best
Discussion to be having while we're waiting
For our friend. For me, of course, it is.
To me it matters very much if he too ...   1600
Listen Daja! – Someone's at our door.
Suppose it's he! Just listen!

Scene 2

Recha, Daja and the Templar
(*Someone has opened the door for the Templar with the words:*)
Come this way.

RECHA   (*Starts, composes herself and is about to fall at his feet*)
It is he! – My saviour!

TEMPLAR   It was to avoid this
That I did not come before. But –

RECHA   At
The feet of this proud man, I just want, once   1605
Again, to thank God; not to thank the man.
The man does not want thanks; he wants them just
As little as the water pail which worked
So hard in putting out the fire. It let
Itself be filled and emptied with no thought   1610
For you or me. The man is like that too.
He too was simply thrust into the blaze;
And quite by chance I stayed there in his arms,
As if I were a spark upon his cloak.   1615
Until something – who knows what? – at last
Propelled us from the blaze. Is this a cause
For thanks? In Europe wine is capable
Of spurring men to every kind of deed.
It's just that Templars sometimes have to act   1620/1
Like this. Like rather well-trained dogs they must
Retrieve things out of fire or out of water.

TEMPLAR   (*who has been watching her in uneasy astonishment*)
Oh Daja, Daja! Just because at moments

	Of distress and bitterness my temper	
	May have given you offence, why did you pass on	1625
	Every stupid word that I let slip?	
	Daja, your revenge on me was too severe!	
	I hope that from now on you'll represent	
	Me to her better.	

DAJA   But I think, sir, if
I'm right, that all these little stings which pricked   1630
Her heart will not have done you any harm
At all.

RECHA   What? You were in distress? So then
You were more miserly with your distress
Than with your life.

TEMPLAR   My good, sweet child! –
How much my soul is torn between my eyes   1635
And ears! – You can't have been the girl, no, no,
It cannot have been you I rescued from
The fire. For how could anyone who knew you
Not have saved you from the fire? Who would
Have waited for me? – Yet – fear changes things.   1640
(Pause while he seems lost in thought, looking at her)

RECHA   And yet I find that you are still the same –
(Pause, until she goes on, to stop him looking at her)
Now, Sir, perhaps you'll tell us where you've been
So long? And I might also dare to ask –
Where are you now?

TEMPLAR   I am – where I perhaps
Should not be.

RECHA   Where were you before? Perhaps   1645
Again where you should not have been? That is
Not good.

TEMPLAR   On – on – what is the mountain called?
On Sinai.

RECHA   On Sinai? – Oh good!
At last I can find out for certain whether
It is true.

TEMPLAR   What? Whether it is true   1650
That you can see there still the place where Moses
Stood before God,[57] where –

---

[57]   Exodus 19:2–3. 'They were come unto the desert of Sinai ... and Moses went
up unto God and the Lord called unto him out of the mountain.'

RECHA   No, no, not that.
Wherever Moses stood, he stood before God.
I know that well enough already. And
I only wanted you to tell me whether   1655
It is true that climbing up that mountain
Is far less difficult than climbing down?
You see, whenever I have tried to climb
A mountain, it was just the opposite.
Well, Sir? – What? – You turn away, and will not   1660
Look at me?

TEMPLAR   Because I want to hear you.

RECHA   Just because you don't want me to see you
Smile at my naiveté. You smile
Because I cannot find a more important
Thing to ask about this holiest   1665
Of mountains? Am I right?

TEMPLAR   In that case I
Must look again into your eyes. But what
Is this? Now you look down, and hide your smile
From me? When I'm only trying to read
In your expression, which is so ambiguous,   1670
What I can hear so clearly, what is audible
In what you say or don't say, – Recha, Recha!
How right he was to say – "Just get to know her".

RECHA   Who was right? Who said that to you?

TEMPLAR   "Get
To know her first", your father said to me,   1675
About you.

DAJA   Isn't that what I said too?
Exactly what I said?

TEMPLAR   But where is he?
Where is your father then? Is he still with
The Sultan?

RECHA   I expect so.

TEMPLAR   He's still there?
Oh how could I forget! No, no. He's most   1680
Unlikely to be there. He will be waiting
For me by the monastery. Of course.
That's what we agreed, I think. Forgive me!
I shall go and fetch him.

DAJA   That's my job.
Stay here, knight. I shall bring him back at once.   1685

TEMPLAR   Oh no. He is expecting me to come,
           Not you. And he might easily – who knows? –
           He might easily at Saladin's –
           You don't know the Sultan – he might well
           Get into trouble. So there's danger if   1690
           I stay, believe me.

RECHA   Danger? But what danger?

TEMPLAR   Danger for me, for you, for him, if I
           Don't go this minute. *(Exit)*

Scene 3

Recha and Daja

RECHA   What has happened, Daja? –
           Why so quickly? What's come over him?
           Why's he rushing off?

DAJA   Just let him go.   1695
           I think it's no bad sign.

RECHA   A sign? Of what?

DAJA   That something's going on inside him. It
           Is simmering, but it must not boil over.
           Leave him. Now it's your turn.

RECHA   My turn? You
           Are as mysterious as he is.

DAJA   Soon   1700
           You will be able to repay him for
           The unrest which he caused you. But you won't
           Be too severe, too full of thoughts of vengeance?

RECHA   I suppose you know exactly what you mean.

DAJA   Have you calmed down so much already. Recha?   1705

RECHA   Yes, I have, I have …

DAJA   At least admit
           To me that you are pleased by his unrest.
           The calmness which you now enjoy is owed
           To his unrest.

RECHA   I'm not aware of that.
           The most I can admit to you is that   1710
           It does seem very strange to me to find
           That such a storm within my heart should be
           So quickly followed by such stillness. Now
           His whole appearance, and his speech, his tone,
           Have …

DAJA   Satisfied you straight away?

| RECHA | I won't | 1715 |

RECHA   I won't   1715
Say satisfied – no – not by a long way –

DAJA   Only calmed the burning hunger.

RECHA   Yes,
You could say that.

DAJA   But I don't.

RECHA   I shall
Always treasure him, more dearly than
My life; although my pulse no longer races   1720
When I hear his name, although my heart
No longer beats with greater speed and vigour
When I think of him. But why this chatter?
Come, dear Daja, come back to the window
Which looks out on to the palms.

DAJA   Your burning   1725
Hunger is not yet entirely stilled.

RECHA   Now I shall see the palms again, not just
The man who walks beneath them.

DAJA   But this coldness
May be just the start of a new fever.

RECHA   What coldness? I'm not cold. Truly I see   1730
With no less pleasure what I can see calmly.

Scene 4

Saladin and Sittah
(Scene: An audience room in the Sultan's palace)

SALADIN   *(as he comes in, standing by the door)*
Bring the Jew in here when he arrives.
He doesn't seem to be in any haste.

SITTAH   Perhaps he was not there, could not be found
At once.

SALADIN   Oh Sister! Sister!

SITTAH   You behave   1735
As if you're ready for a battle.

SALADIN   One
With weapons which I have not learned to use.
To play a part, to make someone afraid,
Set traps for him, to lead him on thin ice.
When could I do that? When ever did   1740
I learn to do it? What is it all for?
What for? To fish for money! Just for money,
To scare a Jew and make him give me money!

For that I'm to resort to petty tricks,
All for the sake of the most trivial   1745
Of trifles?

SITTAH   Every trifle takes revenge
If you despise it, brother.

SALADIN   Sad, but true.
Suppose this Jew should really be the good
And reasonable man described to you
By Al-Hafi recently.

SITTAH   And if he is?   1750
There's no need for trickery. The snare
Is for a Jew who's anxious, miserly
And fearful, not for such a good, wise man.
He's already ours without the snare.
And there's some pleasure in observing how   1755
A man like that can extricate himself.
Whether he can quickly tear the rope
Apart with his audacious strength, or how
He will manoeuvre cunningly to wriggle
Past the net; this is a pleasure which   1760
You'll have in any case.

SALADIN   That's true. Of course
I'm looking forward to it.

SITTAH   So there's nothing else
To worry you at all. For if he's just
Like all the others, if he's no more than
A Jew, like any other Jew, you need not   1765
Be ashamed of seeming just as he
Thinks all men are. Besides in his eyes someone
Who appears to be a better man
Is just an ass, a fool.

SALADIN   And so my bad
Behaviour will prevent a bad man thinking   1770
Badly of me?

SITTAH   If you call it bad,
To use a thing according to its nature.

SALADIN   You women always make your wily plans
Seem better than they are.

SITTAH   What do you mean?

SALADIN   But I'm afraid my clumsy hands will break   1775
So fine and delicate a scheme. It must
Be executed as it was conceived:
With cunning and dexterity. However

That may be, I'll dance as best I can,
And I would rather do it worse than better. 1780

SITTAH Do not underestimate yourself!
I know you'll win, if only you're determined.
Men like you would so much like to make
Us think that your success in life depends
Upon your sword, your sword and nothing else. 1785
When he goes hunting with the fox, the lion
Is ashamed – but of the fox, not of
His cunning.

SALADIN   And a woman always likes
To drag men to her level! Leave me now.
I think I've learned my lesson well enough. 1790

SITTAH What? Must I go?

SALADIN   Did you intend to stay?

SITTAH If not to stay – at least where I can see –
Here in the ante-room.

SALADIN   To eavesdrop there?
Not even that, my sister, if I'm to
Succeed. Now go! The curtain rustles; here 1795
He comes! Don't linger there. I shall be watching.

*(While she goes through one door, Nathan comes in the other and
Saladin has sat down)*

Scene 5

Saladin and Nathan

SALADIN Come closer, Jew – closer – right up to me.
Don't be afraid.

NATHAN   That's for your enemies!

SALADIN You call yourself Nathan?

NATHAN   Yes.

SALADIN   The wise Nathan?

NATHAN No.

SALADIN   You may not; but the people do. 1800

NATHAN The people! Possibly.

SALADIN   You surely don't
Believe that I despise the people's voice?
For some time now I've wished to meet the man
Whom all the people call the Wise.

NATHAN   And if
They call him that in mockery? If wise 1805

	Means to the people nothing more than shrewd,	

Means to the people nothing more than shrewd,
And shrewd just means aware of his own interest.

SALADIN You mean his own *true* interest, I presume?

NATHAN Then the most selfish man would be the shrewdest.
Then shrewd and wise would be the same.

SALADIN   I hear   1810
You proving what you wish to contradict.
Humanity's true interest, which the people
Cannot understand, *you* understand.
At least you've tried to understand it.
You have reflected on it. That alone   1815
Makes a man wise.

NATHAN   But everybody thinks
He's wise.

SALADIN   That's quite enough of modesty!
To hear this all the time when what I seek
For is sober reason fills me with disgust.
(He gets up quickly)
Now let's come straight to the point. But, first of all   1820
Be honest with me, Jew! Be honest!

NATHAN   Sultan
You can rely on me. I'll serve you, and
Prove worthy of your further patronage.

SALADIN You'll serve me? How?

NATHAN   I promise you the best
Of everything, and at the cheapest price.   1825

SALADIN What are you talking about? Surely not
About your goods? My sister may well haggle
With you sometime. (That's in case she's listening!)
I have no business with you as a merchant.

NATHAN In that case, I expect you want to know   1830
What news about the enemy I gathered
On my travels. It is true the enemy
Is active once again, and to be frank ...

SALADIN No, that was not my aim in meeting you.
I know already everything I need   1835
To know of that. – In short –

NATHAN   Command me, Sultan.

SALADIN I want your teaching on another subject.
Something quite different. Since you are so wise,
Tell me, what kind of faith, what kind of law
Has seemed most plausible to you?

NATHAN   Sultan,   1840/1
              I am a Jew.
SALADIN   And I a Muslim. And
              The Christian is between us. Of these three
              Religions only one can be the true one.
              A man like you does not remain, where chance   1845
              Of birth has cast him: if he does, he stays
              From insight, reason, choice of what is best.
              So, share with me your insight. Let me hear
              The reasons which I haven't had the time
              To ponder for myself. Tell me the choice   1850
              Determined by these reasons – in the strictest
              Confidence, you understand – so I
              Can make that choice my own. I see you hesitate.
              You look me up and down. It may well be
              That no Sultan has ever had this kind   1855
              Of whim before. And yet it does not seem
              Unworthy of a Sultan. Do you think?   1857/8
              Speak! – or do you want a moment to   1859/60
              Collect your thoughts? Very well, you may.
              (I'll go and see if Sittah's listening
              And hear if I've done it right.) Now think!
              Think quickly. And I'll soon be back.

              (He goes into the ante-room where Sittah went)

Scene 6
Nathan
              (Nathan alone)
NATHAN   How strange!   1865
              How do I stand? What does the Sultan want?
              I come expecting money. And he wants
              The truth. The truth! and wants it so – straight out.
              In cash, – as if it were a coin! If it
              Were ancient coinage, valued by its weight –   1870
              That might have passed. But such new kinds of coin
              Valued by their stamp, which you must count
              Out on a board, are not like truth at all.
              Can truth be counted out into our heads
              Like money in a sack? Now who's the Jew? –   1875
              He or I? And yet I wonder. Is
              He truly searching for the truth at all?
              Should I suspect that he is only using
              Truth to trap me? That would be too petty.
              Too petty? Nothing is too petty for   1880
              A great man. And, of course he rushed right in,

Like someone bursting through the door. But when
You're visiting a friend, you knock and listen
First. I must be on my guard. But how?
I can't insist that I'm a Jew; but to   1885
Deny that I'm a Jew would be still worse.
Then he could simply ask, "If not a Jew,
Why not a Muslim?" That's it! That can save me!
It's not just children who can be fobbed off
With fairy tales. He's coming. Let him come!   1890

Scene 7

Saladin and Nathan

SALADIN   (And so the coast is clear) – I hope I've given
            You enough time for reflection. Have
            You finished ordering your thoughts? Speak!
            Not a soul can hear us.

NATHAN   I don't mind
            If the whole world were to hear us.

SALADIN   Nathan   1895
            Is so certain of his case? That's what I call
            A wise man! One who never hides the truth.
            A man who, for its sake, will gamble everything
            His blood and land, life and limb.

NATHAN   Yes, if it's needed and of use.

SALADIN   I hope   1900
            I may in future earn the right to bear
            One of my titles: "The Reformer of the World
            And of the Law."

NATHAN   A truly splendid title!
            But before I tell you all my thoughts,
            Sultan, would you allow me to relate   1905
            A little tale?

SALADIN   Why not? I've always loved
            To listen to a story, if it is
            Well told.

NATHAN   I must confess I'm not the man
            To tell it very well.

SALADIN   Your pride and modesty
            Again! Go on, just tell the story, now.   1910

NATHAN   Once long ago, a man lived in the East
            Who had a ring of priceless worth, a gift

From someone dear to him. The stone was opal,
Shot through with a hundred lovely colours.
The ring had secret power to gain favour[58]   1915
In the sight of God and humankind[59]
For anyone who wore it and who trusted
In its power. No wonder that the man
Would never take it from his finger; and
He made provision that the ring should stay   1920
Forever in his dynasty. And so
He left it to the dearest of his sons,
With firm instructions that he, in his turn,
Should leave it to the son he loved the most.
In this way, by the power of the ring,   1925
Without respect of birth, the dearest son
Should always be the master of the house.
You understand me, Sultan?

SALADIN   Yes, go on!

NATHAN   And so the ring passed down from son to son,
Until it reached a father of three sons.   1930
All three alike were dutiful to him.
And he was therefore bound to love all three
Sons equally. And yet, from time to time,
When each in turn was with him on his own,
And did not have to share his overflowing heart   1935
With his two brothers, then the one who stood
Before him seemed most worthy of the ring.
And thus by loving weakness he was led
To promise it to each of them in turn.
So matters rested for a while, until   1940
The father's death drew near; and then the worthy
Man was in a quandary. He could
Not bear to hurt two of his sons, who'd trusted
In his word. So what was he to do?
He sent in secret for a craftsman who   1945
Was ordered to devise two further rings,
Exactly on the pattern of his own,
Whatever cost or effort was required,
To make each ring precisely like the first.
The craftsman did well. When he brought the rings   1950

---

[58]   Luke 2:52. 'And Jesus increased in wisdom and stature and in favour with God and man.'

[59]   (and I Samuel 2:26).

The father was unable to distinguish
The original. With joyful heart
He called his sons, but each one on his own.
To each he gave his blessing and his ring.
And then he died. – You hear me, Sultan?

SALADIN   *(turns away disconcerted)*   Yes,   1955
I hear! – Just finish off your fairy tale.
I hope you're near the end.

NATHAN   That is the end.
It's obvious what follows. Scarcely had
The father died, than each comes with his ring,
And each one claims to be the master of   1960
The house. There are enquiries, arguments,
Complaints. In vain. There was no way to prove
Which ring was true.
(After a pause in which he waits for the Sultan's answer)
                          Almost as hard as now
For us to prove the one true faith.

SALADIN   Is this
To be the answer to my question?

NATHAN   I   1965
Apologize – I cannot trust myself
To tell the difference between the rings,
Because the father had them made precisely
So that no one could distinguish them.

SALADIN   The rings! – Don't play with me! I should have thought 1970
That the religions which I named to you
Were easy to distinguish. Even by
Their clothing; even down to food and drink.

NATHAN   But not the grounds on which they rest.
For are they not all based on history,   1975
Handed down or written? History
We take on trust, on faith. Is that not true?   1977/8
In whose good faith can we most put our trust?
Our people's, those whose blood we share, and who,   1980
From childhood on have proved their love for us,
Who never have deceived us, save, perhaps,
When it was good for us to be deceived?
Can I believe less in my ancestors
Than you believe in yours? Or vice versa,   1985
Can I demand of you that you accuse
Your own forebear of lies, just so that I
Don't contradict my own? – or vice versa.   1988/9
The same is true of Christians, isn't it?   1990

SALADIN	(Upon my life! The man is right.	
	I must be silent.)	
NATHAN	Let us now come back	
	To our three rings. I said before: the sons	
	Accused each other, each swore to the judge	
	He had received his ring directly from	1995
	His father's hand – and it was true. – And he'd	
	Been promised by his father long ago	
	That one day he would have the privileges	
	Of the ring – and that was also true.	
	The father, each declared, could not have been	2000
	So false to him; and rather than allow	
	Suspicion of deceit to fall on his	
	Beloved father; he preferred to charge	
	His brothers with deceit, although he would	
	In general believe only the best	2005
	Of them; and vowed that he would find a way	
	To expose the traitors and to take revenge.	
SALADIN	And what about the judge? I want to hear	
	What you will make him say to this. Go on!	
NATHAN	The judge pronounced: Unless you bring your father	2010
	Here to me at once, I shall dismiss you	
	From my court. Do you think that I am here	
	For solving riddles? Or do you expect	
	For the one true ring to speak up for itself?	
	But wait! You tell me that the true ring has	2015
	The magic power to make beloved; to	
	Gain favour in the sight of God and humankind.	
	That must decide it! For the false rings cannot	
	Have this power. Which brother do two	
	Of you love most? Come on, speak up! You're silent?	2020
	Do the rings work only inwards and	
	Not outwards? So that each one only loves	
	Himself the best? All three of you are then	
	Deceived deceivers; none of your	
	Three rings is genuine. The one true ring	2025
	Has probably been lost. To hide the loss,	
	As substitute, your father had three rings	
	Made to replace the one.	
SALADIN	Splendid! Splendid!	
NATHAN	And so the judge went on, if you do not	
	Want my advice instead of judgement, go!	2030
	But my advice is this: accept the case	
	Precisely as it stands. As each of you	

Received his own ring from his father's hand,
Let each believe for certain that *his* ring
Is the original. Perhaps the father   2035
Did not want to suffer any more
The tyranny of one ring in his house.
Certainly he loved all three of you,
And loved you equally. He could not injure
Two of you and favour only one.   2040
Well then! Let each one strive to emulate
His love, unbiased and unprejudiced.
Let each one of you vie with the other two
To bring to light the power of the stone
In his own ring. And may this power be helped   2045
By gentleness, sincere good nature,
Charity and deepest of devotion to God.
And when in time, the power of the stone
Shall find expression in your children's children's
Children, I invite you in a thousand,   2050
Thousand years to come again before
This court. A wiser man than I will then
Sit in this chair and speak. Now go! – so said
The modest judge.

SALADIN   God! God!

NATHAN   Saladin,
If you should feel yourself to be this promised, 2055
Wiser man …

SALADIN   *(who rushes to him and seizes his hand and does not let go again*
          until the end)
                        I who am no more than dust?
          Than nothing? God!

NATHAN   What is it Saladin?

SALADIN   Nathan, my dear Nathan! The thousand,
          Thousands years of your wise judge have not
          Yet passed. His judgement seat is not the one
          On which I sit. Go! – Go! – But be my friend. 2060

NATHAN   And is there nothing more that Saladin
          Would say to me?

SALADIN   Nothing.

NATHAN   Nothing?

SALADIN   Nothing
          At all. Why do you ask?

NATHAN   I'd like the chance
          To ask a favour of you.

SALADIN	Do you need	
	A chance to ask a favour of me? Speak!	2065

NATHAN   I've come from a long journey during which
I was collecting debts. And now I find
I've almost too much ready money. Times
Are once again becoming troubled, and,
I do not know where I can put it safely.   2070
So I thought that you might possibly, –
Because one needs more money when a war
Is near – that you could use some of it.

SALADIN   *(looking him straight in the eyes)*   Nathan –
I won't ask you if you've just had a visit
From Al-Hafi. And I won't enquire   2075
If some suspicion leads you to propose
This offer of your own accord.

NATHAN   Suspicion?

SALADIN   I deserve that. Please forgive me. What's
The use? I must admit to you – that I
Was just about to …

NATHAN   Surely not to ask   2080
This very thing?

SALADIN   Indeed I was.

NATHAN   So that
Would help us both! – But I must tell you that
I cannot send you *all* my ready cash
Because of the Knight Templar. This young man
Is known to you, I'm sure. My debt to him   2085
Is great, and I must pay it first.

SALADIN   A Templar?
Surely you don't think of giving money
To support my deadliest enemies?

NATHAN   I'm speaking only of this one, whose life
You spared.

SALADIN   Ah, what do you remind me of?   2090
For I had quite forgotten this young man …
You know him? Tell me, where is he?

NATHAN   You mean
You're unaware how much the mercy which
You granted him has flowed through him to me?
He risked his life, which you had newly spared,   2095
In rescuing my daughter from a fire.

SALADIN Did he do that? He seemed that sort of man.
My brother would have done the same, and this
Man so resembles him. Is he still here?
Do bring him! – I have often told my sister   2100
Of this brother whom she never knew.
And now I really cannot let her miss
This chance to see his likeness, in the flesh.
So go, and fetch him! – See how, out of one
Good deed, which sprang from nothing more than passion, 2105
Many more good deeds can flow. Go fetch him!

NATHAN *(releasing Saladin's hand)*
Yes, this minute! And the other matter?
We're agreed on that? *(Exit)*

SALADIN   I should have let
My sister listen – I must go to her!
But how can I explain all this to her?   2110
(Exit on the other side)

Scene 8

Templar alone
(Scene: under the palm trees near to the monastery, where the Templar is waiting for Nathan)

TEMPLAR *(walking up and down, wrestling with himself until he bursts out)*
The sacrificial victim[60] stops exhausted –
So be it! I don't want to understand
What's going on within me; nor to sense
What's going to happen. All I know is that
I fled in vain. In vain! – But what else could   2115
I do but flee? – Well, what will be, will be.
I could not dodge the blow – it fell too quickly,
Although I had refused so long and hard
To fall beneath it. – To have seen this girl
Whom I had wanted so much *not* to see –   2120
To see her and resolve that I could never
Take my eyes from her again. Resolve?
Resolve means purpose, action. Whereas I,
I merely suffered passively. To see her
Was and is to feel entwined to her,   · 2125
Bound up with her. – To live apart from her
Is utterly unthinkable. It would
Be death to me – wherever we may be

---

[60] Jewish and Islamic, not Christian, ritual.

When we are dead, it would be death there too.
If this is love, then certainly a Templar   2130
Is in love, and certainly a Christian
Loves a Jewish girl. What of it? In
The promised land[61] – so full of promise now
For me! – I've cast off many prejudices.
What can my Order want of me? As Templar   2135
I am dead, and have been from the moment
That I became the Sultan's prisoner.
And could this head, a gift from Saladin,
Still be my old one? No, this head is new,
Quite ignorant of all the old one heard   2140
The bonds which held me. And this one is better,
Far more suited to my father's native skies.
That I can sense. For only with this head
Do I begin to think the way my father
Must have thought when he was here – unless   2145
I've been deceived by fairy tales about him.
Fairy tales? Perhaps. But credible,
And never more so than they seem now, when
I am at risk of stumbling where he fell.
Fell? I would rather fall with men, than stand   2150
With children. His example makes me sure
Of his approval. Whose approval do
I need apart from his? Nathan's? I need
Encouragement from him more than approval.
I cannot do without it. What a Jew! –   2155
And yet content to seem a Jew and nothing
Else. But here he comes in haste, his face
Aglow with joy, like everyone who comes
From Saladin. Hey Nathan!

Scene 9

Nathan and the Templar

NATHAN   Ah, it's you!

TEMPLAR You stayed a very long time with the Sultan.   2160

NATHAN Not really very long. I was delayed
        Before I went. I must say, Curd, the man
        Deserves his fame. His fame is just his shadow.

---

[61] Exodus III 8. And I am come down to deliver them out of the land of the
Egyptian and to bring them up out of that land unto a good land and a large,
unto a land flowing with milk and honey.

But he wants me first of all to tell you
Quickly …

TEMPLAR   What?

NATHAN   He wants to speak to you,   2165
And you're to go to him without delay.
But first come home with me, where I must
Deal with some other business for him,
And then we'll go!

TEMPLAR   Nathan, I cannot set foot
In your house again until …

NATHAN   So you   2170
Have been there in the meantime? And
You've spoken to her? – Well then? Tell me, how
Does Recha please you?

TEMPLAR   More than I can say!
And yet, to see her once again – No, never!
Never! Not until you promise, here   2175
And now, that I can see her always, and
For ever.

NATHAN   How do you expect me to
Interpret that?

TEMPLAR *(after a short pause suddenly embraces him)*
                        My father!

NATHAN   But young man!

TEMPLAR *(just as suddenly stepping back)*
            Not son? I beg you, Nathan …

NATHAN   Dear young man!

TEMPLAR Not son? – but, Nathan, – I implore you, I   2180
Beseech you by the earliest bonds of nature! –
Do not be more swayed by later ties –
Just be content with being human. – Don't
Push me away.

NATHAN   My dear, dear friend …

TEMPLAR   And son?
Not son? Would you not even call me son   2185
If in your daughter's heart her gratitude
Had already prepared the way to love?
Not even then, if both were just awaiting
Your signal to be melted into one?
You say nothing?

NATHAN You surprise me, young knight. 2190

TEMPLAR I surprise you? I surprise you, Nathan,
With your own thoughts? – But you don't mistake them
When I put them into words myself?
I surprise you?

NATHAN I don't even know
Your father's place in the Von Stauffen family. 2195

TEMPLAR What are you saying, Nathan? Can it be
That in this moment you feel nothing more
Than curiosity?

NATHAN You see, I knew
A man called Stauffen long ago myself.
His name was Conrad.

TEMPLAR Well – and what if my 2200
Own father's name was also Conrad?

NATHAN Really?

TEMPLAR I was named after my father. Curd
Is Conrad.

NATHAN But my Conrad cannot be
Your father. For my Conrad was, like you,
A Templar Knight, and he was never married. 2205

TEMPLAR Even so.

NATHAN What!

TEMPLAR Even so he could
Have been my father.

NATHAN This must be a joke!

TEMPLAR And you are taking it too seriously.
So what? A bastard, illegitimate!
That's nothing to despise. But kindly spare me 2210
Any more research into my ancestry.
And in return I'll leave yours well alone.
It's not as if I have the slightest doubt
Of your ancestral tree. No, God forbid!
You can authenticate it, leaf by leaf, 2215
Right back to Abraham. And further back
I know it and could swear to it myself.

NATHAN You're bitter. But do I deserve it? Have
I yet refused you anything? It's just
That I don't want to hold you to your word 2220
Immediately – no more than this.

TEMPLAR   You're sure?
           No more than this? Forgive me!

NATHAN   Come, just come!

TEMPLAR   Where? – Not to your house. No! Not there. Not there!
           There's a fire in there. I'll wait here for you. Go!
           If I'm to see her once again, I'll see her   2225
           Often. But if not, then I've already
           Seen far too much of her.

NATHAN   I'll hurry back. *(Exit)*

Scene 10

The Templar and Daja

TEMPLAR   Enough, more than enough! The human brain
           Takes in an almost infinite amount,
           Then suddenly it's full. Just one small thing   2230
           And suddenly it's full! And then it's useless,
           Quite useless, whatever fills it. – But be patient.
           The soul begins to knead the swollen mass,
           To shape it, and to clear some room, then light
           And order come again. Am I in love   2235
           Now for the first time? Or was what I thought
           Was love, not love at all? – And is love only
           What I'm feeling now?

DAJA   *(who has slipped in from the side)*
                                  Oh knight, sir knight!

TEMPLAR   Who's calling? – Daja, so it's you?

DAJA   I have
           Slipped past him. But he still might see us there   2240
           Where you are standing. So come closer to me
           Over here, and hide behind this tree.

TEMPLAR   But what's the matter? Why this secrecy?

DAJA   Yes, it is a secret, which has brought
           Me here to you; in fact a double one.   2245
           Only I know one, and only you
           The other – so how would it be, if we
           Exchanged them? You trust me with yours, then I'll
           Trust you with mine.

TEMPLAR   With pleasure. – If I knew
           What you suppose my secret is. But I   2250
           Expect that will be clear from yours. So you
           Begin.

DAJA   You think so? No, sir knight; first you,
        Then I shall follow. I assure you that
        My secret won't be any use at all
        To you if I don't have yours first. Come on!   2255
        For if I find it out by asking you,
        You'll not have told me anything. And then
        My secret stays my secret, while you've let
        Yours out. Poor knight! How can you men believe
        That you can keep a secret of this nature   2260
        From us women!

TEMPLAR   One that we don't know
        We have ourselves.

DAJA   That may be so. In that case
        I must prove my friendship to you and
        Enlighten you about it. Tell me, sir,
        What was the reason that you rushed away   2265
        From us so suddenly? Why did you leave
        Us sitting there? Why didn't you come back
        With Nathan? Did our Recha make so little
        Mark on you? Or was it all too much?
        Too much! Too much! Now tell me all about   2270
        The little bird, stuck on the lime twig, fluttering!
        In short; confess to me, that you're in love,
        That you're in love with her – madly in love.
        And I'll tell you something …

TEMPLAR   Madly? Yes,
        You understand it very well.

DAJA   Then just   2275
        Admit the love to me; and I'll forget
        The madness.

TEMPLAR   But the madness is quite plain –
        A Templar Knight should love a Jewish girl!

DAJA   There doesn't seem much sense in it, that's true. –
        Yet sometimes there is more of sense in things   2280
        Than we suppose; and after all it would
        Not be so strange if Christ our Saviour drew
        Us to himself on paths that prudent men,
        Left to themselves, would hesitate to take.

TEMPLAR So solemn? (And if I put 'Providence'   2285
        Instead of Christ, is she not right?) – You make
        Me much more curious than I am used
        To being.

DAJA	Oh, this is the land of miracles!	
TEMPLAR	(At least of the miraculous. And how	
	Could it be otherwise, when, after all,	2290
	The whole world crowds together here.) Dear Daja,	
	I confess to you the thing you ask:	
	That I love her, that I can't imagine	
	How I'll live without her, and that I ...	
DAJA	You're sure, quite sure? Then swear to me that you	2295
	Will make her yours, to save her – yes to save her	
	In this world and in eternity.	
TEMPLAR	And how? – How can I? – Can I swear what does	
	Not lie within my power?	
DAJA	But it does	
	Lie in your power. I shall put it in	2300
	Your power with a single word.	
TEMPLAR	You mean	
	Her father will agree to it?	
DAJA	The father!	
	He will have to do so.	
TEMPLAR	Have to, Daja?	
	But he's not yet fallen among thieves –	
	He must not *have* to.	2305
DAJA	Well, then he must want to.	
	Must be glad to in the end.	
TEMPLAR	He must?	
	And gladly? Daja, if I tell you that	
	I have already tried myself to touch	
	This chord in him?	
DAJA	What? Did he not agree?	
TEMPLAR	He did, but with a dissonance which was	2310
	Offensive to me.	
DAJA	Are you telling me	
	That when you let him glimpse the slightest hint	
	Of your wish for Recha, he did not	
	Leap up for joy? But that he drew back	
	Frostily? And that he began to make	2315
	Difficulties?	
TEMPLAR	Yes, something like that.	
DAJA	Then I'll not hesitate a moment longer –	
	(Pause)	

TEMPLAR   You're still hesitating.

DAJA   He is so good
Otherwise. And I owe him so much.
But the fact is that he will not listen.   2320
God knows, my heart bleeds to compel him to.

TEMPLAR   Once and for all, I beg you, Daja, put me
Out of this uncertainty. But if
You are still doubtful whether you should call
What you are planning good or evil, shameful   2325
Or laudable, say nothing. I'll forget
That you have something to conceal.

DAJA   That spurs
Me on instead of stopping me. Well, then,
Recha is no Jew; she is – a Christian.

TEMPLAR   *(coldly)*
So? Congratulations! Was the labour   2330
Hard? Don't let the birth pangs daunt you. Keep on
Propagating heaven's population
If you can't achieve the same on earth.

DAJA   What? Does my news deserve this ridicule?
That Recha is a Christian causes you,   2335
A Christian, and a Templar Knight who loves
Her, no more joy than that?

TEMPLAR   Above all since
She is a Christian of your own creation.

DAJA   Ah! So that is what you thought I meant!
I'd like to see the one who could convert   2340
Her! She was destined long ago to be
What she could not become.

TEMPLAR   Explain or – go!

DAJA   She is a Christian child, of Christian parents,
And she was baptised …

TEMPLAR   *(quickly)*   And Nathan?

DAJA   He is
Not her father.

TEMPLAR   Not her father? Do   2345
You know what you are saying?

DAJA   Just the truth,
Which has so often cost me tears of blood.
No, he is not her father …

TEMPLAR   And he brought
                Her up as if she were his daughter? He
                Brought up this Christian child to be a Jew?   2350

DAJA   Yes, that's exactly what he did.

TEMPLAR   And does
                The girl not know what she was born? Has she
                Not ever learned from him that she was born
                A Christian, not a Jew?

DAJA   No, Never!

TEMPLAR   So
                Not only did he raise the child in this   2355
                Delusion, but he also let her stay
                Deluded, as she grew?

DAJA   Alas!

TEMPLAR   Oh Nathan!
                How? How could the wise, good Nathan have
                Allowed himself to falsify the voice
                Of nature in this way? To lead astray   2360
                The feelings of a heart which, left alone,
                Would take an altogether different path?
                You have indeed confided to me, Daja,
                Something of importance – and which may
                Have consequences – which confuses me –   2365
                I don't know what to do. So go, and give
                Me time to think. He'll come past here again.
                And might surprise us. Go now!

DAJA   That would kill me!

TEMPLAR   I am really quite incapable
                Of speaking to him now. So if you see him,   2370
                Tell him we shall meet each other at
                The Sultan's palace.

DAJA   But don't let him notice
                Anything. This is for you to press
                The matter as a last resort, and to
                Remove all scruples you may have concerning   2375
                Recha. But I hope that if you take
                Her home with you to Europe, you will not
                Leave me behind?

TEMPLAR   We'll see. No, go, just go!

Act IV

Scene 1

The Lay Brother and the Templar
(Scene: In the cloisters of the monastery)

LAY BROTHER Yes, yes, no doubt the Patriarch is right!
    And yet I really wasn't able to   2380
    Succeed in all that he commissioned me
    To undertake. Why does he only give
    Me things like this to do? I cannot be
    So subtle, cannot be persuasive, cannot
    Stick my nose in everywhere, or have   2385
    A hand in everything. And was this why
    For my own sake, I left the world behind,
    Only to find myself involved in worldly
    Matters for the sake of others?

TEMPLAR   *(coming quickly up to him)*   Ah!
    Good brother! There you are. I have been looking   2390
    For you.

LAY BROTHER   Me, sir?

TEMPLAR   You don't recognise me?

LAY BROTHER Yes of course, sir. But I thought that I
    Would never in my life encounter you
    Again. Indeed I hoped to God that I
    Would not. God knows how bitter to me was   2395
    The proposition which I was obliged
    To bring to you. He knows if I sincerely
    Wished to find in you a ready ear.
    He also knows how greatly I was pleased,
    Sincerely pleased, that you turned down outright   2400
    With little hesitation, everything
    That is improper for a knight.
    But now you've come, so it had some effect.

TEMPLAR You know already why I've come? I scarcely
    Know myself.

LAY BROTHER   You've thought it over, and   2405
    Have now concluded that the Patriarch
    Was not so wrong at all; that wealth and honour
    Can be gained by his proposal; that
    An enemy is still an enemy
    Though he may be our saviour seven times.   2410
    You've weighed it up in human terms and come
    To offer your acceptance – ah, dear God!

TEMPLAR	My dear and pious man! Be reassured	
	I have not come for this. I do not want	
	To speak about it to the Patriarch.	2415
	On this I still think as I thought before	
	And I don't want, at any price, to lose	
	The good opinion with which such an upright,	
	Such a pious man, has honoured me.	2419/20
	I've simply come to ask the Patriarch's	
	Advice about a matter.	

LAY BROTHER   You? To ask
                   The Patriarch? A knight has come to ask
                   A priest?
                   (Looking round nervously)

TEMPLAR   Yes, it's a rather priestly matter.

LAY BROTHER	Yet a priest would never ask a knight's	2425
	Advice, however much it was a matter	
	For a knight.	

TEMPLAR	But that's because the priest	
	Enjoys the privilege of doing wrong,	
	Which those like me do not much envy him.	
	Of course, if I were only acting for	2430
	Myself, and if I were accountable	2430
	To no-one but myself, what need would I have	
	Of your Patriarch? In certain things	
	I'd rather do what's wrong, according to	
	The will of others, than what's right according	
	To my own. Besides, I see now that	2435
	Religion too is partisan; however	
	Impartial anyone may think himself,	
	Unconsciously he's bound to stand up for	
	His own cause. Since that's how things are, perhaps	
	That's how they should be.	

LAY BROTHER	Sir, I couldn't say.	2440
	I do not really understand you.	

TEMPLAR	Yet –	2440
	(Let me consider what I really want:	
	To be commanded or advised? Advised	
	By honesty or learning?) Thank you, brother	
	Thank you for your hint. – Why ask the Patriarch?	
	You be my Patriarch! Indeed I want	2445
	To ask the Christian in the Patriarch	
	More than the Patriarch in the Christian.	
	My question is …	

| LAY BROTHER | No more, sir, please no more! |

It's pointless. – You mistake me, sir – The man
Who knows a lot has many cares, and I
Have pledged myself to but a single care.[62]
Good! Listen! Look! He's here, and I'm in luck.
Stay here. He has already noticed you.

Scene 2

The Patriarch who enters with all the pomp of a religious procession, the
Lay Brother, and the Templar

TEMPLAR   I wish I could avoid him. This is not
My man. A rosy, fat and amicable   2455
Prelate! And what pomp!

LAY BROTHER   And you should see him
Setting out for court. Now he has only
Come back from visiting the sick.

TEMPLAR   He must
Put Saladin himself to shame!

PATRIARCH   *(coming closer, beckons to the Lay Brother)*
Come here!
That is the Templar, isn't it? What does   2460
He want?

LAY BROTHER   I do not know.

PATRIARCH   *(going up to the Templar, while his followers and the Lay Brother
draw back)*
Well now, sir knight!
I'm very pleased to see a fine young man.
So very young! Now, with the help of God
Something may come of this.

TEMPLAR   But hardly more,
Your Reverence, than is already there,   2465
And maybe rather less.

PATRIARCH   I wish at least
That such a pious knight may bloom and flourish
For beloved Christianity,
The honour and the service of God's cause!
And that can hardly fail, if youthful courage   2470
Is prepared to follow the mature
Advice of age. How else, sir, may I be
Of service to you?

---

[62] As a Lay Brother he had made a vow only of obedience.

TEMPLAR	With the very thing	
	In which my youth is lacking: with advice.	

PATRIARCH   Most gladly. But advice must be accepted.   2475

TEMPLAR   Yet not blindly?

PATRIARCH   Who says that? Of course
No one must neglect to use the reason
Given him by God – wherever it
Is fitting – but is reason always fitting?
Not at all! For instance, when God, acting   2480
Through one of his angels – that's to say,
Through any servant of his word – is pleased
To show to us a means by which we may
Advance the welfare of all Christendom,
And help the church's cause in some specific   2485
Way, and strengthen it – who then should dare
To use his reason to examine the
Authority of him who first created
Reason? And to scrutinise the eternal
Law of Heaven's majesty, according   2490
To the petty rules of futile honour?
But enough of this. What is the question,
Sir, about which you are seeking our
Advice?

TEMPLAR   Suppose, most venerable father,
That there were a Jew who had a child,   2495
An only child, let's say a girl, and brought her up
With utmost care and goodness; whom he loved
More than his soul, and who in turn loved him
With most devoted love. And then it was
Revealed to one of us that this young girl   2500
Was not the daughter of the Jew. He may
Have come across her as a child, he may
Have bought her, stolen her, or what you will.
And it is known that she's a Christian child
Who was baptised; the Jew has only brought her up   2505
To be a Jew, and has allowed her to
Remain a Jew as his own daughter; tell
Me, venerable father, in this case,
What should be done?

PATRIARCH   I am appalled. But first
Of all, sir, tell me whether such a case   2510
Is actual fact or mere hypothesis?
That is to say – is this your own invention,
Nothing more, or did it really happen
And is still continuing?

TEMPLAR	I should
	Have thought that, to obtain your Reverence's 2515
	View, it would all be the same.

PATRIARCH   The same?

You see, Sir, how the pride of human reason
Can err in spiritual things. – Quite wrong!
For if the case which you have just described
Is just an intellectual game, it does 2520
Not merit serious consideration.
I would refer you to the theatre[63] with
It, sir, where pros and cons of such a kind
Might be debated and could win there great
Applause. But if you have not simply mocked 2525
Me, sir, with a dramatic jest, and if
The case is really factual, if it
Is even possible it has occurred
Within our diocese, our own dear city
Of Jerusalem – well then –

TEMPLAR   What then? 2530

PATRIARCH   Why, then the Jew would swiftly undergo
The penalty laid down by papal and
Imperial law for such a sacrilege,
For such a wicked crime.

TEMPLAR   Indeed?

PATRIARCH   It is

A fact that the aforesaid laws lay down 2535
That any Jew who leads astray a Christian
To apostasy[64] – shall burn to death –
Burn at the stake –

TEMPLAR   Indeed?

PATRIARCH   And how much more

A Jew who snatched a helpless Christian child
By force from its baptismal ties. For is 2540
Not everything that's done to children, force –
Excepting what the Church itself may do
To children.

TEMPLAR   But suppose the child might well

Have died in misery, if she had not
Been rescued by the Jew.

---

[63]   A deliberate anachronism on Lessing's part.

[64]   Apostasy – renunciation of the Christian faith.

PATRIARCH   It makes no difference.   2545
                    The Jew shall burn. For it is better that
                    The child should die in misery than that
                    It should be damned eternally by being
                    Saved in such a way. Besides, how can
                    The Jew anticipate the will of God?   2550
                    Our God saves whom he will, without his help.

TEMPLAR   But surely God can save, in spite of him.

PATRIARCH   No difference! The Jew shall burn.

TEMPLAR   But that
                    Concerns me, and especially as it
                    Is said he brought the girl up not in his   2555
                    Own faith, but rather in no faith at all,
                    And taught her neither more nor less of God
                    Than reason finds sufficient.

PATRIARCH   All this makes
                    No difference! The Jew shall burn.
                    For this alone he should be burnt thrice over.   2560
                    What? Let a child grow up without a faith
                    Of any kind? What? Not to give a child
                    The slightest teaching of its greatest duty,
                    Namely to believe? How wicked! I'm
                    Astonished, sir, that you yourself …

TEMPLAR   The rest,   2565
                    Your Reverence, God willing, in confession.
                    (he is about to go)

PATRIARCH   What? You will not tell me now? Not name
                    The Jew, the villain? Not surrender him
                    To me? In that case, I know what to do!
                    I'll go at once to Saladin. The Sultan   2570
                    Must, according to the treaty sworn
                    By him, he must protect us; must protect
                    Us in all laws and in all doctrines which
                    We have the right to claim as ours, as part
                    And parcel of our holiest religion!   2575
                    Praise be to God; we have the document,
                    We have his hand and seal. Yes, that we have!
                    And I can make him understand quite easily
                    The danger to the state itself
                    Of not believing anything. All civil   2580
                    Ties are loosened, torn apart if people
                    Are allowed to have no faith at all.
                    Away, away with such an outrage!

TEMPLAR	I
	Regret that I cannot enjoy this splendid
	Sermon at my leisure. But I have 2585
	Been called to Saladin.
PATRIARCH	To Saladin? Yes? – Well – of course
	– then –
TEMPLAR	I will ensure the Sultan is prepared
	For this, if that's your Reverence's wish.
PATRIARCH	Ah, yes! – I know you have found favour, sir,
	With Saladin. I ask you to remember 2590
	Me to him in the very best of terms.
	I'm driven wholly by my zeal for God.
	And if I go too far, it is for him –
	I hope you will bear that in mind, dear sir.
	And what you said just now about the Jew 2595
	Was nothing more than a debating point?
	That is to say –
TEMPLAR	Just a debating point. *(Exit)*
PATRIARCH	(Which I must thoroughly investigate.
	So this will be another task to give
	To Brother Bonafides) – Here, my son. 2600
	(He talks to the Lay Brother as he goes out)
	(I have another errand for you)

Scene 3

Saladin and Sittah

(Scene: a room in Saladin's palace into which a large number of bags are being carried by slaves and being piled up on the floor.) Saladin is joined by Sittah

SALADIN	*(coming in)*
	Well really, there's no end to this. Is there
	Much more to come?
SLAVE	About as much again.
SALADIN	Then take the rest to Sittah. – And where has
	Al-Hafi gone? Al-Hafi should be taking
	All this money straight away – or had 2605
	I better send it to my father? Here
	It will just slip straight through my fingers. Yet
	One does get hardened in the end; now it
	Will take some skill to get much out of me.
	At least till all the gold from Egypt has 2610
	Arrived, the poor will have to cope as best
	They can. As long as alms can still be given

At the sepulchre, and Christian pilgrims
Do not have to leave with empty hands!
As long as ...

SITTAH   What's all this? What should I do   2615
With all this money?

SALADIN   Pay yourself, and store
The rest, if there is any left.

SITTAH   Has Nathan
Still not come here with the Templar?

SALADIN   No. He
Is looking for him everywhere.

SITTAH   I found
This picture when I was sorting through all my   2620
Old jewels.
(Showing him a small painting)

SALADIN   Ah! my brother! That is him!
Yes, that is him! Or rather, that was him
Ah, dear courageous boy, alas that I
Lost you so soon. What might I have accomplished
If I had had you by my side! – Sittah,   2625
Give me the picture. I remember it;
He gave it to your elder sister, his
Dear Lilla, when one morning she refused
To let him go from her embrace. That was
The last time he rode out. Alas, I let   2630
Him ride out, all alone. – Poor Lilla died
Of grief. She had never forgiven me
For letting him ride out alone like that. –
And he did not return.

SITTAH   Poor brother!

SALADIN   So
Be it. One day we all will go and not   2635
Return. And then – who knows? Not only death
Can turn a young man like him from his goal.
He has more enemies than that; the strongest
Often falls as quickly as the weakest.
Be that as it may! – I must compare   2640
This picture with the young Templar, and see
How far my own imagination has
Deceived me.

SITTAH   That is why I brought it. Give
It to me, and I'll tell you; this is something
Which a woman's eye can judge far better.

SALADIN	*(to a servant who comes in)* Who	2645
	Is there? – the Templar? – Show him in!	
SITTAH	I won't	
	Disturb you – and I won't confuse him with	
	My curiosity.	
	(Sittah sits to one side on a sofa and lowers her veil)	
SALADIN	That's good! – (And now	
	His voice! I wonder what it's like. Within	
	My soul, somewhere the voice of Assad sleeps.)	2650

Scene 4

The Templar and Saladin

TEMPLAR	Your prisoner, Sultan …	
SALADIN	My prisoner?	
	If I grant life to someone shall I not	
	Grant freedom to him also?	
TEMPLAR	It is fitting	
	I should hear what you think fitting, not	
	Anticipate your actions. And yet, Sultan,	2655
	To express my special thanks to you	
	For sparing me is not in keeping with my rank	
	Or with my character. In any case	
	My life is once more at your service.	
SALADIN	Do	
	Not use your life against me! I would gladly	2660
	Grant my enemy another pair	
	Of hands. To grant him such a heart would be	
	More difficult. I've not in any way	
	Misjudged you – you're a fine young man. And you're	
	The very image of my Assad. I	2665
	Might even ask you: where have you been hiding	
	All this time? And in what cave have you	
	Been sleeping?[65] What good spirit, in what fairy	
	Land, has kept this flower so fresh for all	
	This time? Indeed, I could remind you of	2670
	The things we used to do together, you	
	And I. And yet, I could be angry with	
	You, too, for keeping one thing secret from me,	

---

[65]   The legend of the Seven Sleepers tells of seven young people, who would not worship the emperor as god, who were hidden by a shepherd in a cave, which was then sealed up by the emperor. After 186 years they woke up, not having aged.

For there's one adventure which you never
Shared with me. Indeed I could; if I   2675
Saw only you, and not myself as well.
So be it! There remains such truth in this
Sweet reverie that in the autumn of
My days an Assad is alive again.
Are you content with this, knight?

TEMPLAR   Everything   2680
That comes to me from you – whatever it
May be – my soul desires already.

SALADIN   Let
Us test that out. Would you remain with me,
Stay near me? – As a Christian, Muslim – either
In your white cloak or in an Arab robe   2685
With turban or with your felt cap. Just as
You like. It's all the same. I've never wanted
The same bark to grow on every tree.

TEMPLAR   Or you would hardly be the man you are:
A hero who would rather be God's gardener.   2690

SALADIN   Well, if you think no worse of me, we are
Already half agreed?

TEMPLAR   Completely!

SALADIN   *(offering his hand)*   Here's
My hand.

TEMPLAR   *(taking his hand)*
                  And mine – with this, accept far more
Than you could take from me. Now I am yours.

SALADIN   These gains are too much for a single day!   2695
He did not come with you?

TEMPLAR   Who?

SALADIN   Nathan.

TEMPLAR   *(coldly)*
                                            No.
I came alone.

SALADIN   How fine a deed of yours!
And what wise fortune that a deed like that
Should turn out for the good of such a man.

TEMPLAR   Oh, yes.

SALADIN   So cold? – Oh no, young man! When God   2700
Does something good through us, one must not be
So cold! – One must not even wish to seem
So cold from modesty.

TEMPLAR	But in this world
	There are so many sides to everything.
	And often it is difficult to see 2705
	Just how they fit together.
SALADIN	Therefore always
	Keep to the best, and give praise to God,
	Who knows how they all fit together. If
	You wish to be so difficult, young man,
	Then probably I also should be on 2710
	My guard with you. Regrettably
	I am a creature too, of many sides,
	Which often may seem not to fit so well.
TEMPLAR	That hurts! – Suspicion is not usually
	A fault of mine.
SALADIN	Then tell me who gives rise 2715
	To it in you. It seems that it was Nathan.
	You suspect him? Speak, Explain yourself!
	Come give me this first proof of confidence.
TEMPLAR	I have nothing against Nathan. I
	Just blame myself.
SALADIN	For what?
TEMPLAR	For dreaming that 2720
	A Jew could ever quite forget to be
	A Jew. And yet I had this dream when I
	Was wide awake.
SALADIN	What was this day dream? Tell me.
TEMPLAR	You know of Nathan's daughter, Sultan. What
	I did for her, I did – because I did. 2725
	Too proud to harvest any thanks where I
	Had never sown, from day to day I had
	Disdained to see the girl again. The father
	Was away; then he returns, he hears
	About it, finds me, thanks me, hopes that I 2730
	May like his daughter, speaks of prospects, and
	A happy future. He persuades me, so
	I come, I see, and I find truly such
	A girl – oh Sultan, I should be so ashamed!
SALADIN	Ashamed? Because a Jewish girl made an 2735
	Impression on you: surely not!
TEMPLAR	Because
	The father's talk beguiled me, and my rash heart
	Could offer almost no resistance to
	This impression. What a fool I was!

	I jumped into the fire a second time –	2740
	For now *I* wooed and now *I* was disdained.	
SALADIN	Disdained?	
TEMPLAR	Well, the wise father did not flatly	
	Turn me down. The wise father would need	
	To make enquiries first, he needed to	
	Reflect. Of course! Did I not do that too?	2745
	Did I not make enquiries, and reflect	
	While she was screaming in the fire? Indeed!	
	My God! My God! How fine a thing it is	
	To be so wise, and circumspect.	
SALADIN	Come now!	
	You might make some allowance for his age.	2750
	How long do you suppose he can refuse?	
	Do you expect him to demand that you	
	Should first become a Jew yourself?	
TEMPLAR	Who knows!	
SALADIN	Who knows? – A man who knows this Nathan better.	
TEMPLAR	The superstition in which we grew up	2755
	Does not relax its power over us,	
	Not even when we see it as it is.	
	And so, not all who mock their chains are free.	
SALADIN	Yes, how mature! But Nathan, really, Nathan …	
TEMPLAR	And the worst of superstitions is	2760
	To think one's own most tolerable.	
SALADIN	That	
	May be. But Nathan …	
TEMPLAR	To let dull	
	Humanity believe in that alone	
	Till it can take the brighter light of truth;	
	In that alone …	
SALADIN	Agreed. But Nathan, – Nathan	2765
	Does not have this weakness.	
TEMPLAR	So I thought.	
	If none the less this paragon of men	
	Were such a common Jew that he had sought out	
	Christian children so that he could bring	
	Them up as Jews; – what would you think of that?	2770
SALADIN	But who says that of him?	
TEMPLAR	The girl herself	
	With whom he lured me on, as if he wished	
	To pay me with the promise of her for	
	An act which he assumed I didn't do	

	For nothing. The girl is not his daughter – no: 2775 She is a foundling Christian child.
SALADIN	But even So, he did not want to give her to you?

SALADIN

                          But even
So, he did not want to give her to you?

TEMPLAR   *(stormily)*
Whether he did or not! He is unmasked.
This tolerant old windbag is unmasked.
I'll call for dogs to be unleashed upon   2780
This Jewish wolf in philosophical[66]
Sheep's clothing, and they'll tear him limb from limb!

SALADIN   *(sternly)*
Be quiet, Christian!

TEMPLAR   What? Be quiet, Christian?
When Jews and Muslims all insist on being
Jews and Muslims, only Christians may
Not act the Christian?

SALADIN   *(more sternly)*   Quiet, Christian!

TEMPLAR   *(calmly)*   Now
I feel the weight of the reproach compressed
In these two words by Saladin. Ah, if
I knew how Assad – how your Assad would
Have acted in my place!

SALADIN   Oh, not much better!   2790
Probably as violently. But who
Already taught you, just like him, to pierce
Me with a single word? Of course, if everything
Turns out as you have said, then I myself
Can not make Nathan out at all. But in   2795
The meantime he is still my friend, and none
Among my friends must quarrel with another.
Take my advice; proceed with care. Don't give
Him straight to the fanatics in your mob.
Just imagine what your clergy would   2800
Demand from me as a revenge on him.
Do not be a Christian just to spite
A Jew or Muslim.

TEMPLAR   It might soon have been
Too late, but for the Patriarch's blood lust,
Which made me shudder to become his tool.

---

[66] Matthew 7:15. 'Beware of false prophets which come to you in sheep's clothing, but inwardly they are ravening wolves.'

SALADIN   What?   2805
      You went to see the Patriarch, before
      You came to me?

TEMPLAR   Yes in a storm of passion,
      In a whirl of indecision. Please
      Forgive me! From now on I fear you will
      Not want to recognize Assad in me.   2810

SALADIN   Unless I recognize this fear itself!
      I know the faults from which our virtue springs.
      Just practice virtue, and the faults will do you
      Little harm with me. But you must go.
      Now seek out Nathan, as he sought you out;   2815
      And bring him here. I have to make you understand
      Each other. If you're serious
      About the girl, don't worry – she is yours.
      And Nathan also must be made to pay
      For having dared to rear a Christian child   2820
      Without the taste of pork.[67] Now go!
      (*The Templar goes out and Sittah leaves the sofa*)

Scene 5

Saladin and Sittah

SITTAH   How strange!

SALADIN   Admit it, Sittah; don't you think my Assad
      Must have been a handsome, fine young man?

SITTAH   If he was really like that, and the Templar
      Did not sit as model for this portrait!   2825
      But Saladin, how could you have forgotten
      To enquire about his parents?

SALADIN   In
      Particular about his mother, whether
      She had ever visited this country –
      Is that what you mean?

SITTAH   You could have asked.   2830

SALADIN   It's certainly quite possible. For Assad
      Was so welcome among pretty Christian
      Ladies, was entranced by Christian ladies,
      That there even was a rumour – well,
      One doesn't like to talk about it. It's   2835
      Enough I have him back – and want him back
      With all his faults, with all the changing moods

---

[67]   Eating pork is forbidden both by Jewish and Islamic religions.

Of his warm heart. Oh, surely Nathan must
Give him the girl. Don't you agree?

SITTAH   Give her?
Give her up!

SALADIN   Indeed. What kind of right   2840
Could Nathan have to her, if he is not
Her father? Only one who saved her life
Has rights to her, inherited from one
Who *gave* her life.

SITTAH   Well Saladin? Suppose
You have the girl brought here to you? Remove   2845
Her straight away from her unlawful owner.

SALADIN   Is that really necessary?

SITTAH   Not
Exactly necessary. Curiosity
Alone makes me suggest it to you.
With certain men I want to know as soon   2850
As possible the kind of girl with whom
They are inclined to fall in love.

SALADIN   Then, send
For her, and have her brought here.

SITTAH   May I, brother?

SALADIN   But spare Nathan's feelings. He must not
Believe that we intend to tear the girl   2855
From him by force.

SITTAH   Don't worry.

SALADIN   And meanwhile
I must find out what's happened to Al-Hafi.

Scene 6

Nathan and Daja

(Scene: the hall in Nathan's house, opening on to the palms; as in the first scene. Part of the goods and treasures are lying around unpacked as they are being sorted out)

DAJA   Oh, this is all so splendid! Exquisite!
Oh, everything – as only you can give.
Where do they make this silver cloth with interwoven   2860
Gold? What does it cost? That's what
I call a bridal dress! No queen could ask
For better.

NATHAN   Bridal dress? Why bridal dress?

DAJA	Of course you did not think of that when you
	Were buying it. But truly, Nathan, it 2865
	Must be this one and nothing else. It is
	As if intended for a bride. The white
	Background, symbol of innocence; the golden
	Threads which twist and turn all over it,
	Symbol of riches. Look at it: it's lovely! 2870
NATHAN	What are you telling me? Whose bridal dress
	Are you interpreting so learnedly?
	Are you the bride?
DAJA	I?
NATHAN	Who then?
DAJA	I? Dear God!
NATHAN	But who? Whose bridal dress are you describing?
	This is all for you and no one else. 2875
DAJA	All this is mine? For me? And not for Recha?
NATHAN	What I bought for Recha is still packed
	Inside another bale. Go on! Away!
	Take all your bits and pieces!
DAJA	Oh you tempter!
	No. If this were all the treasure of 2880
	The whole wide world. I wouldn't touch it, Not
	Unless you swear to me that you will use
	This unique opportunity, which heaven
	Will not offer you a second time.
NATHAN	Use what? – An opportunity for what? 2885
DAJA	Oh, don't pretend that you don't know – in short,
	The Templar Knight loves Recha; give her to him,
	By doing so, at once you end your sin
	Which I cannot keep secret any longer.
	The girl will be with Christians once again, 2890
	Will once again be what she is; and once
	Again be what she was. And you, whom we
	Can never thank enough for all your goodness,
	At last you will escape the coals of fire[68]
	Upon your head.
NATHAN	Again the same old song? 2895
	But you have fixed a new string to your lyre,
	Which will not hold or stay in tune, I fear.

---

[68]   Romans 12:20. 'Therefore if thine enemy hunger feed him, if he thirst give him drink, for in so doing thou shalt heap coals of fire on his head.'

DAJA	Why not?
NATHAN	The Templar is a good man, and To no one in the world would I prefer To give my Recha, but – have patience.
DAJA	Patience?　2900 Isn't patience just the same old song From you?
NATHAN	Just patience for a few more days! But look – who's that approaching? It's a lay brother Go, and ask him what he wants.
DAJA	What can he want? *(She goes and asks him)*
NATHAN	Before he asks, just give him alms – (If　2905 I could only sound the Templar Knight out first And not tell him the reason why I ask. For if I tell him and there are no grounds For my suspicion, I have put the father Needlessly at risk.) What does he want?　2910
DAJA	He wants to speak to you.
NATHAN	Well, let him come: And meanwhile you can go.

Scene 7

Nathan and the Lay Brother

NATHAN	(If only I Could still be Recha's father! – Can't I be, Even when I cease to bear the name? She herself will always call me father　2915 If she sees how much it means to me.) What service can I do you, holy brother?
LAY BROTHER	Very little. – Nathan, sir, I'm pleased To see you are still well.
NATHAN	You know me then?
LAY BROTHER	Indeed; who doesn't know you? You have pressed　2920 Your name into the hands of many people. It has remained in mine for many years.
NATHAN	*(reaching for his purse)* Come, brother, come; I will refresh it.
LAY BROTHER	Thank you, I'd be stealing from a poorer man, So I'll take nothing. But allow me to　2925 Refresh your memory about my name.

For I can pride myself on having put
Into your hands something of no mean worth.

NATHAN   Forgive me. – I am ashamed – what was it, tell
Me? And accept as penance sevenfold   2930
The value of this thing from me.

LAY BROTHER   But first
Of all, just listen how, this very day,
I was reminded of this pledge I had
Entrusted to you.

NATHAN   You entrusted me?

LAY BROTHER Not long ago I lived a hermit's life   2935
On Quarantana[69] near to Jericho.
There came an Arab band of robbers, who
Destroyed my little temple and my cell
And carried me off with them. Luckily
I fled, and came here to the Patriarch   2940
To beg another small place for myself
Where I could serve my God in solitude
Until my days should reach a peaceful end.

NATHAN   I burn to know the rest. Good brother, make
It brief. The pledge! The pledge entrusted me!   2945

LAY BROTHER At once, sir. – I was promised by the Patriarch
A hermit's cell on Tabor,[70] just as soon
As one was free; meanwhile I was to stay
As a lay brother in the monastery.
I am there now, Nathan sir; and yearn   2950
A hundred times a day for Tabor. For
The Patriarch makes use of me for many
Things which are repugnant to me, for
Example:

NATHAN   Please go on.

LAY BROTHER   I'm coming to it –
Somebody today has whispered to   2955
Him that a Jew is living somewhere here
Who has brought up a Christian child as his
Own daughter.

---

[69] Quarantana, a mountain between Jericho and Jerusalem whose name refers
to the 40 days and 40 nights of Christ's temptation in the wilderness.

[70] Tabor, a mountain in Galilee, associated with the transfiguration of Christ.

NATHAN   (*Taken aback*)   What?

LAY BROTHER   Just, just let me finish. Then
            He orders me to run this Jew to earth
            Without delay, if possible, and he   2960
            Condemns most vehemently such a crime
            Which is, it seems to him, the very sin
            Against the Holy Ghost[71] – that is the sin
            Which, of all sins, is counted by us as
            The greatest; but thank God we don't exactly   2965
            Know what such a sin consists of. Then
            My conscience suddenly awakes and it
            Occurs to me that, long ago, perhaps
            I gave the opportunity for this
            Great, unpardonable sin. So tell   2970
            Me: eighteen years ago did not a groom
            Bring you a little girl a few weeks old?

NATHAN   What? – Yes, that's true – I do admit –

LAY BROTHER   Well then,
            Just look at me. I am that groom.

NATHAN   You are?

LAY BROTHER The gentleman from whom I brought her was –   2975
            If I remember right – a Herr von Filnek –
            Wolf von Filnek.

NATHAN   Right!

LAY BROTHER   The mother had
            Just died, and suddenly the father had
            To hurry off – I think to Gaza,[72] where
            The little thing could not go with him. So   2980
            He had her sent to you. Did I not meet
            You with her in Darun?[73]

NATHAN   Quite right.

LAY BROTHER   It would
            Be little wonder, if my memory
            Deceived me. I've had many worthy masters,
            And I served this one all too short a time.   2985

---

[71] Matthew 12:31. 'The blasphemy against the Holy Ghost shall not be forgiven unto men.'

[72] Gaza was recaptured from the Crusaders by Saladin.

[73] Darun – on the Palestinian border near to Egypt.

Soon after that he died at Askalon;[74]
He was a kindly gentleman.

NATHAN   Indeed.
I have so very much to thank him for,
Since more than once he saved me from the sword.

LAY BROTHER That's very good. So you'd have taken in   2990
His little daughter very willingly.

NATHAN   You can be sure I did.

LAY BROTHER   Then, where is she?
I hope it cannot be that she has died?
Oh let her not have died. For if there's no-one
Else who knows about it, – then some good   2995
May come of it.

NATHAN   It may?

LAY BROTHER   Trust me, Nathan!
Listen, this is what I think. If I
Intend to do a good deed, but a deed
Which borders closely on the bad, then I   2999/0
Would rather leave the good undone. Because
We can be sure of knowing what is bad,
But we are far less sure of what is good.
It was of course quite natural that if
The little Christian girl was to be well   3005
Brought up by you, you raised her as your daughter
And you would have done it with all love
And true devotion. So is this how you
Should be rewarded? I cannot believe so.
Of course it might have been more prudent if   3010
You had arranged to have the Christian child
Brought up by someone else, as Christian; but
You would in that case have denied your love
To your friend's child. And children at that age
Need love, if only that of a wild beast,   3015
More than they need Christianity.
Christianity can wait till later.
So long as, in your eyes, the girl has grown
To be devout and healthy, in the eyes
Of God she has remained just as she was.   3020
And was not all of Christianity
Founded on Judaism? It has often
Caused me pain, and cost me many tears,

---

[74] Askalon – a coastal town taken by Saladin in 1187.

| | That Christians could so utterly forget | |
| | That our dear saviour was a Jew. | 3025 |

NATHAN   Good brother, you must be my advocate
            If hatred and hypocrisy are roused
            Against me – all because of such a deed –
            Ah, such a deed! Now you alone shall know
            About it. Take it with you to the grave!   3030
            Vanity has never tempted me
            To speak of it to anyone. To you
            Alone, I'll speak, to you and to your simple
            Piety. For only such a one
            Can understand what deeds can be achieved   3035
            By human beings who submit to God.

LAY BROTHER You're deeply moved; your eyes are full of tears.

NATHAN   In Darun you met me with the child.
            But you don't know that, only days before,
            In Gath,[75] the Christians murdered all the Jews, 3040
            Their wives and children; and you do not know
            That in this number were my wife and, with
            Her, seven sons, all full of promise. In
            My brother's house, where I had sent them to
            Be safe, they burned to death.

LAY BROTHER   Almighty God!   3045

NATHAN   When you arrived, three days and nights, in dust
            And ashes, I had lain before my God
            And wept. But more than wept, I argued bitterly
            With God, I stormed, I raged, I cursed myself
            And all the world, and swore undying hate   3050
            Of Christendom at large.

LAY BROTHER   That I believe.

NATHAN   And yet my reason gradually returned.
            It spoke with gentle voice: 'Yet God exists.
            And even this was God's decree. And so,
            Arise and act the way you long have understood; 3055
            It surely is not harder now to act
            Than it has been to understand, if you
            But have the will. Stand up!' – And so I stood,
            And cried to God, 'I will! If only you
            Can will me to it.' At that moment, you   3060
            Dismounted from your horse, and handed me
            The child wrapped in your cloak. What passed between

---

[75] Gath – on the Mediterranean coast.

Us I forget. But this I know: I took
The child, I put it on my couch, and kissed it
Fell upon my knees and sobbed: 'Oh God!   3065
For seven, one is now restored!'

LAY BROTHER   Oh Nathan!
You're a Christian! Yes, by God, a Christian!
A better Christian there has never been!

NATHAN   It works both ways. For what makes me a Christian
In your eyes, makes you a Jew in mine.   3070
But enough of all our feelings. We
Need action! And although my love already
Binds me seven fold to this one foreign
Girl, although the thought already kills me
That I must lose my seven sons again   3075
In her – if providence demands that I
Surrender her again, – I shall obey.

LAY BROTHER Now that's exactly the advice I had
In mind to offer you. But now your own
Good spirit has already said the same.   3080

NATHAN   But I can't let anyone who comes
Along tear her from me.

LAY BROTHER   Of course not.

NATHAN   One
Who has no greater rights to her than I
Must at the least have earlier rights –

LAY BROTHER   Of course.

NATHAN   Rights granted him by nature and the ties   3085
Of family.

LAY BROTHER   Yes, I agree.

NATHAN   So quickly
Name the man related to her – brother,
Uncle, cousin, other relative;
I won't refuse her to him – for she was
Created and brought up to be the pride   3090
Of any house, of any faith. I hope
That you know more than I about this man
Who was your master, and his family.

LAY BROTHER Good Nathan, I'm afraid I hardly do!
I have already told you that I served   3095
Him only very briefly.

NATHAN   Do you not
At least have any knowledge of the mother's
Family? – Was she perhaps a Stauffen?

LAY BROTHER Possibly! – I think so.

NATHAN   Was her brother
              Not Conrad von Stauffen, a Knight Templar?   3100

LAY BROTHER If I'm not mistaken. Yes. But wait.
              I think I still possess my master's little
              Book which he kept by his heart. I took
              It when we buried him in Askalon.

NATHAN   Yes?

LAY BROTHER A book containing prayers – what we call   3105
              A breviary. This, I thought, could still
              Be useful to a Christian – not to me,
              I cannot read.

NATHAN   That doesn't matter. Carry
              On.

LAY BROTHER   At the beginning and the end
              Of this small book, so I've been told, are written,   3110
              In the gentleman's own hand the names
              Of both the families.

NATHAN   Just as I hoped!
              Go quickly! Bring the book to me. But run!
              I'll offer you the weight of it in gold,
              Together with a thousand thanks; be quick!   3115

LAY BROTHER With pleasure. But my master's writing is
              In Arabic. (*Exit*)

NATHAN   It doesn't matter, bring it!
              Oh God! If I could only keep the girl
              And gain a son-in-law like him as well!
              It's hardly likely. Well then, let things turn   3120
              Out as they will. But who can it have been
              Who brought this matter to the notice of
              The Patriarch? I must remember to
              Investigate. Could it have been Daja?

Scene 8

Daja and Nathan

DAJA   (*in a hurry and embarrassed*)
              Just imagine Nathan!

NATHAN   What is it?   3125

DAJA   The poor child was quite terrified by it!
              They've sent for her …

NATHAN   The Patriarch?

DAJA	The Sultan's Sister, Princess Sittah …
NATHAN	Not the Patriarch?
DAJA	No, Sittah! – Don't you hear me? – Princess Sittah Sent for her. She wants to see her.
NATHAN	Who? 3130 She sent for Recha? – Sittah sent for her? Well then, If Sittah sends for her, and not The Patriarch …
DAJA	Why mention him?
NATHAN	So you've Heard nothing from him recently? You're sure? You've told him nothing?
DAJA	I? Tell him?
NATHAN	Where are 3135 The messengers?
DAJA	Outside.
NATHAN	For safety's sake I'll speak to them myself. Just come! – I hope The Patriarch is not behind all this. *(Exit)*
DAJA	And I – I have a different fear. What's going On? A girl who is supposed to be 3140 The only daughter of a wealthy Jew Would be no bad match for a Muslim? – Oh, The Templar's chance is lost. He's lost, unless I venture now upon the second step, And tell the girl herself just who she is. 3145 I must! As soon as I can talk to her Alone, I'll grasp the opportunity. And that will be – perhaps right now, when I Go with her. On our way at least I'll drop A hint to start with. That can do no harm. 3150 Yes, yes, it's now or never! I must speak. *(Exit)*

Act V

Scene 1
Saladin and Mameluke[76]
  (*Scene: The room in Saladin's palace into which the sacks of money have been carried – which are still to be seen*)

SALADIN (*as he comes in*)
  The money is still here, and no one yet
  Knows where the Dervish is – presumably
  He's found a chessboard somewhere, and that always
  Seems to make him forget himself; –   3155
  So why not me? I must be patient. Yes?

MAMELUKE The news you hoped for, Sultan. Joyful news –
  The caravan from Cairo has arrived,
  It's safely here, and brings you seven years
  Of tribute from the wealthy Nile.

SALADIN   Good, Ibrahim!   3160
  You are indeed a welcome messenger.
  At last! It's here at last! My thanks to you
  For the good news.

MAMELUKE (*waiting*)   (Well? Come on, hand it over!)

SALADIN Why are you waiting? You may go.

MAMELUKE   You give
  Me welcome, nothing else?

SALADIN   What else?

MAMELUKE   The welcome   3165
  Messenger gets no reward? – So Saladin
  Has learned to pay with words, and I'm the first
  To benefit? That's fame, to be the first
  He treated meanly.

SALADIN   Well then, take a sack
  Of money for yourself.

MAMELUKE   Not now. Not even if   3170
  You gave me all of them.

SALADIN   Defiance! Come,
  Take two of them. He means it? Now he's gone,
  Surpassing me in generosity,
  Although for him it must be harder to   3175
  Refuse it than for me to give. Come back!

---

[76] Mameluke – member of the Sultan's bodyguard.

What has come over me so near my death
That suddenly I want to change my nature?
Does Saladin refuse to die as Saladin?
Then he should not have lived as Saladin.

MAMELUKE 2   Greetings, Sultan.

SALADIN   If you've come to tell me ...   3180

MAMELUKE 2   That the caravan from Egypt has arrived.

SALADIN   I know already.

MAMELUKE 2   Then I came too late.

SALADIN   And why too late? – Here for your good intentions
You can take a sack or two.

MAMELUKE 2   Ah, one
Or two makes three!

SALADIN   So you can count? Just take
them.   3185

MAMELUKE 2   There may be a third man coming – that is
If he's able.

SALADIN   Meaning what?

MAMELUKE 2   Well now;
It's possible he has a broken neck; because
As soon as we, the three of us, were sure
The convoy had arrived, we galloped off.   3190
The one who was in front fell off his horse.
Then I was in the lead, and stayed there till
We came into the town, where Ibrahim,
The rogue, has better knowledge of the streets.

SALADIN   But what about the one who fell, my friend?   3195
Ride out and meet him.

MAMELUKE 2   Yes I will. And if
He's still alive, I'll give him half the money.
(*Exit*)

SALADIN   He's a good and noble fellow too.
Who else can boast of Mamelukes like these?
And may I not believe that they are what
They are, at least in part, from my example?   3200
I must reject the thought of changing that
Example as I end my days.

MAMELUKE 3   Sultan!

SALADIN   You're
The one who fell?

MAMELUKE 3	No. I come to report
	That Emir Mansor, who led the caravan 3205
	Is now dismounting from his horse.
SALADIN	Quick! Bring
	Him here. Ah, here he is.

Scene 2

Emir Mansor and Saladin

SALADIN	You are most welcome.
	Emir. How did it go? Mansor, Mansor,
	You have kept us waiting for so long!
MANSOR	This letter tells you what kind of unrest 3210
	In Thebes[77] your Abukassem had to quell
	Before we dared to set off on our way.
	After that, I forced the pace as much
	As possible.
SALADIN	Yes, I believe you, Emir.
	Now, good Mansor – and I know you'll do 3215
	It gladly – you must take fresh escort straight
	Away. And you must leave again at once,
	And take the bulk of all this money to
	My father in the Lebanon.
MANSOR	Yes, gladly.
	Very gladly.
SALADIN	Be sure to take 3220
	Sufficient escort. It's no longer safe
	In Lebanon. Have you not heard? The Templars
	Are in action once again. Be on
	Your guard. Now, where's the camel train? I want
	To see it and take care of everything 3225
	Myself. You there! I'll be with Sittah later.

Scene 3

The Templar
> (*Scene: the palms in front of Nathan's house where the Templar is pacing up and down*)

TEMPLAR	I won't set foot inside the house again –
	He must appear eventually. They welcomed
	Me so eagerly before, and now
	I'm likely to be told that he no longer 3230

---

[77] In upper Egypt.

Tolerates my presence all the time
Outside his house. And yet I also feel
Provoked to anger. What has so embittered
Me against him? – After all he said,
He didn't yet refuse me anything. 3235
The Sultan promised to persuade him – what
Then? Is it that the Christian in me is
More deeply rooted than the Jew in him?
Who really knows himself? Why else should I
Be so reluctant to allow the little 3240
Theft which he committed for his purposes
Against the Christians. But this is no little
Theft of such a creature! Creature? Who
Is her creator? Not the slave, who floated
The unhewn block on to the barren shore 3245
Of life, and then ran off. No, it must surely
Be the artist who, in the abandoned block,
Conceived a godly form and fashioned it.
Truly, Recha's real father must
Remain, despite the Christian who begot 3250
Her, must remain the Jew forever. If
I think of her as just a Christian girl,
And think of her devoid of everything
Which only such a Jew could give to her,
Then, my heart, what would you see in her? – 3255
Almost nothing! For her smile itself
Would be a sweet and gentle movement of
The muscles, nothing more. And if what made
Her smile was never worthy of its charm upon
Her mouth, I would not even like her smile. 3260
I have seen sweeter, wasted on mere whims
And useless trifles, scorn and flattery,
Flirtation – and did those enchant me too?
Did they too conjure up the wish in me
To flutter all my life away in their 3265
Sunshine? Oh no. And yet I'm angry with
The man who, single-handed, made her what
She is. But why? Perhaps I merited
The scorn with which I was dismissed by Saladin.
It's bad enough that Saladin should think so. 3270
How small I must have seemed to him! And how
Contemptible! And all this for a girl? –
Curd! Curd! This cannot be. Control yourself!
Suppose that Daja was just chattering
About a thing that would be difficult 3275
To prove? At last! He's coming from his house.

He's deep in conversation. But with whom?
With him, with my Lay Brother? Ah! so now
He must know everything! Perhaps he is
Betrayed already to the Patriarch.   3280
Oh what a fool I've been to cause all this,
To think that just a single spark of passion
Can set all our brain on fire! Now quickly
Make your mind up: What are you to do?
I'll wait here for them, to one side – perhaps   3285
The Brother will be leaving before long.

Scene 4

Nathan and the Lay Brother

NATHAN   *(as they approach)*
          Once again, good brother, many thanks.

LAY BROTHER My thanks to you as well!

NATHAN   Your thanks for what?
          Because I obstinately pressed on you
          Something you don't need? If only you   3290
          Had given in. But you refused to be
          A richer man than I am.

LAY BROTHER   Anyway,
          The book does not belong to me. It is
          The daughter's property. In fact
          The one and only legacy she has   3295
          From her own father – though she does have you.
          God grant you never may have reason
          To regret all you have done for her.

NATHAN   How could I?
          Never! Have no fear of that.

LAY BROTHER   And yet,
          With all these Patriarchs and Templar Knights ...   3300

NATHAN   No harm that they could ever do to me
          Would make me feel regret for anything
          I've done, and certainly not this.
          And are you sure it really is a Templar
          Who's stirring up your Patriarch?

LAY BROTHER   It couldn't   3305
          Have been anybody else. A Templar
          Had just been talking to him; what I heard
          Confirmed it.

NATHAN   But at present there is only
          One of them in all Jerusalem.

I know him, and he is a friend of mine,   3310
A noble and sincere young man!

LAY BROTHER   That's right,
The very one! Yet what one is and what
One must be in this world – the two things don't always
Fit exactly.

NATHAN   Sadly not; and so
Whoever it may be, just let him do   3315
His worst or best! Now, Brother, with your book
I shall defy them all, and take it straight
To Saladin.

LAY BROTHER   Good luck! I'll leave you now.

NATHAN   You haven't even seen her? Come back soon,
And come as often as you can. I hope   3320
The Patriarch learns nothing more today.
But why not? Tell him if you like.

LAY BROTHER   I shan't.
Farewell! *(Exit)*

NATHAN   But don't forget us, Brother – God!
If only I could sink upon my knees
Right here, under the vault of heaven. How   3325
The tangled web, which caused me such anxiety,
Unravels of its own accord! – Oh God,
How light I feel now that there's nothing that
I need to hide, and now that I can walk
Before humanity as freely as   3330
Before your sight. You are the only one
Who does not judge us human beings by
Our deeds, which rarely are our deeds, Oh God.

Scene 5

Nathan and the Templar
The Templar comes up to Nathan from the side

TEMPLAR   Hey, Nathan, wait! Take me with you.

NATHAN   Who's that?
Oh, there you are! Where did you go? I was   3335
Expecting you to meet me at the Sultan's.

TEMPLAR   We missed each other. Don't be angry.

NATHAN   I am
Not. But Saladin ...

TEMPLAR   You had just left.

NATHAN   You spoke to him? That's good.

TEMPLAR   He wants to speak
          To both of us together.

NATHAN   Better still.   3340
          Come with me. I am on my way to him.

TEMPLAR   May I ask you, Nathan, who it was
          Who left you just now?

NATHAN   Don't you know him then?

TEMPLAR   Wasn't it that good soul, the Lay Brother
          Whom the Patriarch is fond of using   3345
          To sniff things out?

NATHAN   Perhaps. He's in the service
          Of the Patriarch.

TEMPLAR   A clever trick,
          To let a simple man prepare the way
          For villainy.

NATHAN   Yes, if he's stupid – not
          If he is pious.

TEMPLAR   But no Patriarch   3350
          Believes in piety.

NATHAN   I'll vouch for this man.
          He won't help his Patriarch do anything
          Improper.

TEMPLAR   So he claims. But didn't he
          Say anything to you concerning me?

NATHAN   Concerning you? He did not mention you   3355
          By name. He'd hardly know your name.

TEMPLAR   No, hardly.

NATHAN   As it happens, he did speak about
          A Templar …

TEMPLAR   And said what?

NATHAN   He cannot
          Possibly have meant you in this case.   3360

TEMPLAR   Who knows? What did he say?

NATHAN   That someone had
          Denounced me to the Patriarch.

TEMPLAR   Denounced
          You? That is – with all due respect to him –

Not true. Now listen to me, Nathan. I
Am not a man who can deny my deeds.
What I did, I did, and that is that.   3365
And I am not a man who would defend
What I have done as always being right.
Why should I be ashamed of a mistake?
Am I not determined to redeem it?   3370
Do I not know how far a man can go
To put things right? Now listen, Nathan: yes,
I am the Brother's Templar Knight, who is
Supposed to have denounced you; it is true.
Of course you know what made me angry, and
What caused my blood to boil in every vein.   3375
Fool that I was, I came to throw myself
Body and soul into your arms. And your
Reaction was so cold – so lukewarm, which
Is even worse than cold; how carefully   3380
You calculated your evasion of me!
You appeared to want to answer me
By asking questions, plucked out of the air.
I still can hardly bear to think of it
If I'm to keep my head. And then, Nathan,
In this turmoil Daja stealthily   3385
Crept up to me and flung her secret in
My face. This seemed to hold the key to your
Mysterious behaviour.

NATHAN   How was that?

TEMPLAR   Just hear me! I imagined that you were   3390
Unwilling to give up to Christian hands
What you had taken from the Christians in
The first place. So, in short, I then resolved
For good or ill, to hold a knife up to
Your throat.

NATHAN   For good or ill? What good? Where is
The good in that?

TEMPLAR   Just hear me, Nathan. What   3395
I did was wrong. And you are not to blame.
That Daja is a fool who doesn't know
What she is saying, and her spite towards you
Makes her want to get you into trouble.   3400
Perhaps that's true. And I am young and stupid,
Always rushing to extremes of feeling,
Always doing too much or too little.
Perhaps that's also true. Forgive me, Nathan!

NATHAN   If this is what you take me for ...

TEMPLAR   In short,
           I went to see the Patriarch – I did   3405
           Not name you, though – that is a lie, as I
           Have said. I simply told him of the case
           In general terms, and asked for his opinion –
           Of course I should have left it all unsaid.   3410
           I knew already that the Patriarch
           Was villainous. Why couldn't I have talked
           To you at once? Why did I have to let
           The poor girl run the risk of losing such
           A father? But what does it matter now?
           That villain of a Patriarch, who always   3415
           Will remain just as he is, has quickly
           Brought me to my senses. Listen, Nathan,
           Listen to me – let us just suppose
           That he already knows your name. What more   3420
           Can he do? He can only take the girl
           If she belongs to you and no one else.
           And only from *your* house can he remove
           Her to the cloister – so, give her to me!
           Give her to me, and let him come! He surely
           Would not dare to take my wife away.   3425
           Just give her to me; quickly! I don't care
           If she's your daughter, or she's not! And I
           Don't care if she's a Christian or a Jew
           Or if she's neither. I don't care! It's all   3430
           The same. And all my life I'll ask you nothing
           More about it. What will be, will be!

NATHAN   I have such need to hide the truth? You really
           Think so?

TEMPLAR   What will be, will be!

NATHAN   But I
           Have never yet concealed from you – or anyone
           Who ought to know – that she's a Christian, and   3435
           That she is no more than my foster daughter.
           But why, you ask, have I not told her yet?
           For that I need apologize to none
           But her.

TEMPLAR   But you don't even have to do that.
           May she never have to look on you   3440
           With different eyes. Spare her the revelation.
           You and you alone, are still responsible
           For her. Give her to me! I beg

	You, Nathan, just give her to me! I am

You, Nathan, just give her to me! I am
The only one who, for the second time,   3445
Can save her for you – and I will.

NATHAN   I could
Have done so, but not now. It is too late
For that.

TEMPLAR   Too late?

NATHAN   Thanks to the Patriarch.

TEMPLAR   The Patriarch? Thanks? Thanks to him? For what?   3450
He is the one who ought to give us thanks.
So why thank him?

NATHAN   Because we know to whom
She is related, and we know into
Whose hands she now can safely be entrusted.

TEMPLAR   Thank him? Let the devil thank him!   3455

NATHAN   And now you must receive her from those hands,
And not from mine.

TEMPLAR   Poor Recha! How you are
Pursued by fate, poor Recha! What for any
Other orphan would be great good fortune
Is disaster for you. Nathan, where   3460
Are these relations?

NATHAN   Where?

TEMPLAR   And who are they?

NATHAN   They've found a brother in particular,
And you must ask him for her hand.

TEMPLAR   A brother?
What is he, this brother? He's a soldier?
Or a priest? – Just tell me what I can
Expect ....

NATHAN   I think that he is neither, or   3465
Perhaps he may be both. I don't know much
About him yet.

TEMPLAR   What else?

NATHAN   A fine young man.
With whom our Recha may perhaps do well.

TEMPLAR   And yet he is a Christian. Sometimes, Nathan,   3470
I just don't know what to think of you.
I don't mean to offend you, but when she's with

Christians, won't she have to play the Christian?
If she plays it long enough, she'll end
Up really being one, and then the pure
Corn which you sowed will finally be choked   3475
By weeds. And does that worry you so little?
Can you really say, in spite of that,
That with her brother, Recha may perhaps
Do well?

NATHAN   I think so, and I hope so. And   3480
If she lacks anything from him, can she
Not always turn to you and me?

TEMPLAR   Oh, can
She possibly lack anything from him?
The little brother will provide his little
Sister with a rich supply of food
And clothing, sweets and finery. What else   3485
Could such a little sister need? Of course,
A husband! – Well, the little brother, in
His own good time, will certainly provide
Him too; he only has to find him, and   3490
The more Christian the better! Nathan, Nathan!
What an angel you created, just
For others to destroy your work for you.

NATHAN You need not fear that. He will prove to be
Most worthy of our love.

TEMPLAR   Don't say that! Never
Say that of *my* love! For it will not   3495
Be cheated of the slightest thing, however small,
Not even of a name. But tell me, does
She yet have reason to suspect what has
Been happening to her?

NATHAN   Perhaps, I don't   3500
Yet know. Why do you ask me?

TEMPLAR   Just because
I have to be the one to tell her what
Fate threatens her, in either case. I thought
That I would never see or speak to her
Again, until I was allowed to call her
Mine. But all is changed. I'll hurry.   3505

NATHAN   Where?
Come back!

TEMPLAR   To her. To see if, in her soul
This girl is man enough to make the one
Decision which is worthy of her.

NATHAN	What

NATHAN   What
                 Is that?

TEMPLAR   To pay no further heed to you   3510
                 Or to her brother ...

NATHAN   And?

TEMPLAR   To follow me;
                 Even if it meant that she became
                 A Muslim's wife.

NATHAN   But wait! She isn't there.
                 She's with the Sultan's sister.

TEMPLAR   Why? How long
                 Has she been there?

NATHAN   And if you want to meet
                 The brother there as well, just come with me. 3515

TEMPLAR   Whose brother? Sittah's brother? – Recha's?

NATHAN   Both,
                 Perhaps. Just come with me – I beg you, come!
                 (He leads him away)

Scene 6

Sittah and Recha
     (Scene: in Sittah's harem. Sittah and Recha are in conversation.)

SITTAH   How pleased I am that you are here, sweet girl.   3519
           Don't feel oppressed. So anxious, and so shy!   3520
           Be cheerful, more relaxed and talkative.

RECHA   Princess ...

SITTAH   Not princess! ... Please call me Sittah,
           Your friend – your sister. Call me mother, if
           You like. For I could almost be your mother.
           You're so young, so clever and so good!   3525
           You know so much, and must have read so much.

RECHA   I must have read? – Dear Sittah, you make fun
           Of me, your simple little sister. I
           Can scarcely read.

SITTAH   That can't be true! Scarcely?

RECHA   I can read my father's hand a little,   3530
           But I thought that you referred to books.

SITTAH   Yes, books.

RECHA	Well, I find books most difficult
	To read.
SITTAH	You're serious?
RECHA	Quite serious.
	My father has no love of cold book-learning
	Which imprints itself upon the brain 3535
	With lifeless symbols.
SITTAH	How extraordinary!
	But maybe there's some truth in it. So, much
	Of what you know ...
RECHA	I know only from his
	Own teaching. And for most of it I still
	Could tell you how and when and why he taught it 3540
	To me.
SITTAH	Maybe everything makes better
	Sense like this, because the whole soul learns
	At once.
RECHA	I'm sure that Sittah has read very
	Little.
SITTAH	The contrary, though I'm not proud of it.
	Why do you say that? Tell me frankly, why? 3545
RECHA	You are so simple and direct; so natural,
	Like no one but yourself.
SITTAH	And what of that?
RECHA	My father says that people who read books
	Are seldom like that.
SITTAH	What a splendid man
	Your father is!
RECHA	He is.
SITTAH	How near the mark 3550
	He always hits.
RECHA	He does. And yet my father ...
SITTAH	What's the matter, Recha dear?
RECHA	My father –
SITTAH	God! Why are you crying?
RECHA	Oh, my father –
	I must tell you, or my heart will burst ...
	(overcome by weeping she falls at her feet)

SITTAH	My child, what is the matter with you, Recha?	3555
RECHA	I'm going to lose my father!	

SITTAH
          Lose your father?
How? Now, calm yourself. Get up! You'll never
Lose him.

RECHA
      You must have meant it, when you said
That you would be my friend, my sister ...

SITTAH
               Yes,
I did, indeed I did. But please, get up,   3560
Or I shall have to call for help.

RECHA   *(pulls herself together and gets up)*
            Forgive me!
In my grief I was forgetting who
You are. There is no case for whining and
Despair in front of Sittah. She will be
Convinced simply by reason, cool and calm.   3565
And anyone who pleads a cause with reason
Always wins her over.

SITTAH   Well?

RECHA
         Ah, no
My friend, my sister, do not let them. Never
Let them force another father on me.

SITTAH   Force another father on you? Who   3570
Could do that? My dear Recha, who could want to?

RECHA   Who? My Daja, – good and evil as
She is – yes, she could want to, and could do
It. But you probably don't know this good
And evil Daja? God forgive her – and   3575
Reward her! She's done so much good for me,
And so much evil.

SITTAH   Evil? So there can
Be little good in her.

RECHA
          Oh yes, there is,
A great deal.

SITTAH   Who is she?

RECHA
          A Christian who
Looked after me in childhood; you could not   3580
Believe how well she cared for me, so that
I hardly missed my mother. God reward
Her for it! Yet, she also frightened and
Tormented me.

SITTAH	But what about? Why? How?
RECHA	Ah, the poor woman, as I told you, is 3585
	A Christian, so her love made her torment me.
	She is one of those fanatics who
	Imagine that they know the only true
	And universal way to God.
SITTAH	Yes, now
	I understand.
RECHA	They have to lead all those 3590
	Who missed the one true way, and guide them to
	It. They have little choice. For if it's true
	That only this way leads them in
	The right direction, then how could they calmly
	Watch their friends pursue another path 3595
	Which leads them to damnation, eternal
	Damnation. Surely one could love and hate
	A single person simultaneously.
	But it's not that which in the end compels
	Me to complain about her. All her sighs 3600
	And warnings, all her prayers and all her threats,
	I would have tolerated longer – yes.
	They always prompted good and useful thoughts.
	And surely it is deeply flattering
	To us to feel that any fellow-creature 3605
	Loves and values us so much as to
	Be tortured by the thought of losing us
	For all eternity.
SITTAH	That's true!
RECHA	And yet –
	I have no weapon against this, not patience,
	Not reflection, nothing!
SITTAH	Against what? 3610
RECHA	What she claims to have revealed to me
	Just now.
SITTAH	Revealed? Just now?
RECHA	Just now. When we
	Were coming here, as we approached a ruined
	Christian temple, suddenly she stopped.
	She stood, and seemed to struggle with herself. 3615
	With tear-filled eyes she looked up at the heavens,
	Then at me. At last she said, 'Come, let us
	Take the shortest path, right through this temple.'

She led on, I followed her, and I
Looked round with horror at the crumbling ruins.   3620
Then she stopped again. I saw that we were
On the sunken steps before a ruined
Altar. Imagine how I felt when, weeping
Scalding tears, she flung herself down at
My feet, and wrung her hands.

SITTAH   My dearest child!   3625

RECHA   And by the divinity[78] who has received
So many prayers there and, they say, has worked
So many miracles, she pleaded with me;
With a look of true compassion she
Implored me to have mercy on myself.   3630
Or at least to pardon her if she
Now told me of her church's claim on me.

SITTAH   (Unhappy child! – I feared as much.)

RECHA   She said
I was of Christian blood; I was baptised;
I was not Nathan's daughter; he was not   3635
My father. God! God! He is not my father!
Sittah! Sittah! I prostrate myself
Before you.

SITTAH   Recha, no! Get up. – My brother's here.

Scene 7

Saladin and the preceding

SALADIN   What's happened, Sittah?

SITTAH   She's distraught! – Oh God! 3640

SALADIN   Who is it?

SITTAH   But you know ....

SALADIN   Our Nathan's daughter?
What is wrong?

SITTAH   Compose yourself, my child.
The Sultan ...

RECHA   *(drags herself on her knees to Saladin's feet,*
and bows her head to the ground)
I shall not stand up! And I
Shall never look upon the Sultan's face,
And never more admire the image of   3645

---

[78] The Virgin Mary.

	Eternal justice and of goodness in	
	His eyes, and on his brow ...	
SALADIN	Stand up, stand up!	
RECHA	Until he promises ...	
SALADIN	I promise it,	
	Whatever it may be!	
RECHA	No more, no less	
	Than this: to let me keep my father, and	3650
	Let him keep me. – I still don't know who else	
	Demands to be my father, or who has	
	The right. And I don't want to know. Does blood	
	Alone create a father?	
SALADIN	*(raising her up)* Yes, I understand!	
	Who was so cruel as to put such thoughts	3655
	Into your head? But has this matter been	
	Completely settled? Proved beyond all doubt?	
RECHA	It must have been. For Daja claims to have it	
	From my nurse.	
SALADIN	Your nurse!	
RECHA	She felt, as she	
	Was dying, that she must confide in her.	3660
SALADIN	As she was dying – and perhaps delirious?	
	But what if it were true? No: blood, and blood	
	Alone, can never make a father! Hardly	
	Even father of a beast. It gives	
	At most a prior right to claim that name.	3665
	So don't let yourself get anxious. And	
	Do you know what? As soon as these two fathers	
	Quarrel over you – leave both of them	
	And take a third. Accept me as your father!	
SITTAH	Yes! Oh do!	
SALADIN	I'll be a good father.	3670
	A really good father. But wait! An even	
	Better thought occurs to me. Why do you	
	Need a father anyway? What when he dies?	
	You need to look around for someone who	
	Will match you in the race of life. Do you	3675
	Not know someone?	
SITTAH	Don't make her blush!	
SALADIN	That is	
	Exactly what I meant to do to her.	

	If blushing makes the ugly beautiful,	

If blushing makes the ugly beautiful,
It's bound to make the lovely even lovelier.
I've asked your father, Nathan, and – another   3680
Man to join us here. Can you guess who
That is? I've asked him here – with your permission,
Sittah …

SITTAH   Brother!

SALADIN   Now be sure you really
Blush before him, dearest girl.

RECHA   Why should
I blush? For whom?

SALADIN   You little hypocrite!   3685
Turn pale, then, if you like. – Just as you please,
And as you can. –
(A slave girl comes in and goes up to Sittah)

SALADIN   Have they arrived already?

SITTAH   *(to the slave)*
Good. Just show them in. – Brother, they're here!

Last Scene

Nathan and the Templar join the others

SALADIN   My dear, good friends! – and first of all, dear Nathan
I must tell you that you now can ask   3690
For all the money which you lent to be
Repaid, as quickly as you like.

NATHAN   Sultan!

SALADIN   I am at *your* service now.

NATHAN   Sultan!

SALADIN   The caravan has come. And now at last
I'm richer than I've been for many years.   3695
Come, tell me what you need to undertake
Some mighty enterprise! For even merchants
Like yourself can never have enough
Of ready cash!

NATHAN   Why do you mention first
So insignificant a trifle? For I see
Someone in tears. It matters more to me
That I should dry them. *(Goes up to Recha)*
                        You've been crying? What's
The matter? Are you not my daughter still?

RECHA	My father!	
NATHAN	That's enough, we understand	3705
	Each other. Now be calm, be cheerful – if	
	Your heart is still your own, and if your heart	
	Is threatened by no other loss. – Your father	
	Is not lost.	
RECHA	I fear no other loss.	
TEMPLAR	No other? Then, I have deceived myself.	3710
	What we are not afraid to lose, we never	
	Thought that we possessed, and never even	
	Wanted. Very well! In that case, Nathan,	
	All is changed. We came here, Saladin,	
	At your command. But I regret that I	
	Misled you; give yourself no further trouble!	3715
SALADIN	Must you be so rash again, young man?	
	Must everything come back to you, defer	
	To you?	
TEMPLAR	But Saladin, you heard and saw?	
SALADIN	Yes. And it's a pity you were not	
	More certain of your case.	
TEMPLAR	I am now.	3720
SALADIN	Anyone who boasts of a good deed	
	Cancels it right out. What you have saved is not	
	Your property. If that were so, a robber	
	Driven by his greed into a fire	
	Would be as good a hero as yourself.	3725
	(Going up to Recha, to lead her to the Templar)	
	Come, dear girl. Don't be too hard on him.	
	If he were different, less proud and less	
	Impulsive, he would not have tried to save you.	
	You must weigh the one against the other.	
	And now, put him to shame! Do what he should	3730
	Have done. Confess your love. Propose to him!	
	If he refuses you, or if he should	
	Forget that you have done much more for him,	
	By taking such a step, than he has done	
	For you – what did he do for you? He got	3735
	Himself a little smoke-stained? How impressive!	
	Such a man has nothing of my brother,	
	Assad. He may wear his mask, but not	
	His heart. So come, my dear …	

SITTAH	Yes, go, my dear!
	That is the least that you can do to show 3740
	Your gratitude.
NATHAN	Wait, Saladin! Wait, Sittah!
SALADIN	You as well?
NATHAN	There's someone else who has
	To speak.
SALADIN	But Nathan, who denies that such
	A foster father has a right to speak?
	Perhaps a better right than others. I 3745
	Know all about the situation.
NATHAN	Not quite all! –
	I wasn't speaking of myself, but of
	Another, someone else entirely who
	Must be consulted, Saladin.
SALADIN	But who?
NATHAN	Her brother.
SALADIN	Recha's brother?
NATHAN	Yes.
RECHA	My brother? 3750
	So I have a brother?
TEMPLAR	*(starting out of his wild, silent abstraction)*
	Where? Where is
	This brother? Not here yet? I was supposed
	To meet him here.
NATHAN	Yes, just be patient.
TEMPLAR	*(very bitterly)*
	He has
	Imposed a father on her, – so he can
	Supply a brother, can't he?
SALADIN	That's too much! 3755
	Christian! Such a mean suspicion never
	Would have passed my Assad's lips. All right –
	Just carry on.
NATHAN	Forgive him, Sultan!
	– I forgive him gladly. At his age,
	And in his place, who knows what we would think? 3760
	(going up to him in a friendly way)
	Yes, knight, I understand. Mistrust begets
	Suspicion. If you'd only trusted me
	With your real name …

TEMPLAR	What?
NATHAN	You are not a Stauffen.
TEMPLAR	Who am I?
NATHAN	Your name's not Curd von Stauffen.
TEMPLAR	What is it?
NATHAN	You're Leu von Filnek.
TEMPLAR	What? 3765
NATHAN	You're startled?
TEMPLAR	Rightly so. Who says this?
NATHAN	I do;

I could tell you more, much more. But I
Am not accusing you of lying.

TEMPLAR	No?
NATHAN	Perhaps the other name is also yours.
TEMPLAR	I should hope so! – (Just as well you said that!) 3770
NATHAN	Yes, your mother was a Stauffen. And

Her brother – that's your uncle – brought you up.
Your parents left you with him when the harshness
Of the German climate drove them out,
And they returned here to this country. Now, 3775
Your uncle's name was Curd von Stauffen; and
Perhaps he did adopt you as a child.
Was it with him that you also came here,
So long ago? And is he still alive?

TEMPLAR	What can I say to you? Of course, it's true. 3780

My uncle died. I only came here with
The latest reinforcement of our Order,
But – what has all this to do with Recha's
Brother?

NATHAN	Now, your father …
TEMPLAR	What? You knew

Him too?

NATHAN	Your father was my friend.
TEMPLAR	Your friend? 3785

Can it be possible?

NATHAN	And he was known

As Wolf von Filnek; though he was not German.

TEMPLAR	You know this too?
NATHAN	But he was married To a German – that's your mother – and He followed her to Germany, though not 3790 For long.
TEMPLAR	Enough! The brother – who is Recha's Brother?
NATHAN	You are.
TEMPLAR	I? Her brother?
RECHA	He's my brother?
SITTAH	Brother and sister!
SALADIN	Is it possible?
RECHA	*(going to him)* My brother!
TEMPLAR	*(steps back)* Brother?
RECHA	*(stops and turns to Nathan)* No, it can't be true. His heart denies it! – We're deceivers, God! 3795
SALADIN	*(to the Templar)* Deceivers, Templar? Is that what you think? But you are the deceiver! Everything About you – face and voice and bearing – is A lie. You will not recognise your sister? Go!
TEMPLAR	*(going humbly to him)* Sultan, don't misinterpret my 3800 Astonishment. You hardly could have seen Assad at such a moment; don't misjudge Both him and me. *(going to Nathan)* You rob me and enrich me, Nathan; both in fullest measure. But You give me far, far more than you have taken. 3805 *(Embracing Recha)* Oh my sister, my dear sister!
NATHAN	Blanda Von Filnek.
TEMPLAR	Blanda? Blanda? – And not Recha? Not your Recha any more? – You are Rejecting her, by giving back her Christian Name? Reject her if you must, but Nathan, 3810 Why do you make Recha suffer so?

NATHAN   Nonsense! Children! You are both my children!
For my daughter's brother is my son –
If he is willing.
(Leaving them to embrace each other Saladin
goes in uneasy astonishment to his sister)

SALADIN   Sister, tell me what
You think.

SITTAH   I'm moved.

SALADIN   I too – I almost shudder at   3815
The thought of something still more moving. So
Prepare yourself, as best you can.

SITTAH   What do
You mean?

SALADIN   Nathan, a word with you ...
(While Nathan goes to him, Sittah goes up to the
brother and sister to express her sympathy and
Nathan and Saladin talk quietly.)
                  Now listen,
Nathan: did you not just tell us ...

NATHAN   What?

SALADIN   You told us that their father did not come   3820
From Germany, and was not born a German.
So what was he, and where did he come from?

NATHAN   He didn't choose to talk to me about it.
I know nothing that I heard from him.

SALADIN   But he was not a Frank? A Westerner?   3825

NATHAN   No, he was not. He made no secret of it.
He preferred to speak in Persian.

SALADIN   He spoke Persian?
What more do I want? It must be him!

NATHAN   It must be who?

SALADIN   My brother! Assad! There
Can be no doubt!

NATHAN   Now that you've worked it out,   3830
You'll find full confirmation in this book.
(handing him the breviary)

SALADIN   *(opening it eagerly)*
His writing! Yes I recognize that too!

NATHAN   They don't know anything about this. It's
Entirely up to you how much they learn.

SALADIN   *(leafing through the book)*
              Should I not recognise my brother's children?   3835
              My nephew and my niece – my children? Not
              Acknowledge them? And should I let you keep them?
              (aloud again)
              Sittah! I was right! They are, they really
              Are! They are our brother's children!
              (Runs to embrace them)

SITTAH   *(following him)*
                                                    What!
              But then, how could it have been otherwise?   3840

SALADIN   *(to the Templar)*
              Now, stubborn man, you will be forced to love me!
              (to Recha)
              And Recha, I shall be what I offered
              Whether or not you want it!

SITTAH   So shall I.

SALADIN   *(to the Templar again)*
              My son! My Assad! My own Assad's son!

TEMPLAR   So I am of your blood? – And so those dreams   3845
              Which rocked me in my cradle, after all
              Were more than dreams! *(falling at his feet)*

SALADIN   *(raising him up)*
                                      Just listen to the rascal!
              He suspected something, but he did
              His best to make me murder him! You wait!
              *(Silently they all embrace each other again and the
              curtain falls.)*

THE END